THE YAMAHA ADVANTAGE™

Musicianship from Day One

by Sandy Feldstein and Larry Clark
Piano Accompaniment by Carl Strommen

Welcome to the Yamaha Advantage™

The Yamaha Advantage piano accompaniments are designed to make the classroom experience more fun. Use these accompaniments to aid learning for the students and to add excitement when performing. Most lines in the book are included in this collection except for some Advantage exercises. Chord symbols are provided if you would like to add a guitar or to give the accompanist the ability to improvise if desired.

The recorded accompaniments are available separately or downloadable from the Web site. They are based on these piano accompaniments and will provide additional enjoyment for the students.

We would like to thank Carl Strommen for his assistance in the preparation of these accompaniments.

Have a great time making music.

Sandy Feldstein   Larry Clark

CARL FISCHER®
65 Bleecker Street, New York, NY 10012

Graphic System Development, Design and Illustration:
Susan Blakely

YBM121

ISBN 0-8258-4413-4

1 1 #1
Let the Band Begin
F F Gm7 F/A Gm7 F F/A Gm7 F
2 1 #2
It Is All Air
F B♭/F F B♭/F F Gm7 F/A B♭ F/A Gm7 F
3 1 #3
The Second Note
E♭ A♭/E♭ E♭ Fm7 A♭ E♭/G Fm7 E♭/G Fm7 E♭
4 1 #4
More in Four
E♭ A♭ B♭7 A♭/C D° E♭ A♭ B♭7 E♭

5 1 #5

The Third Note

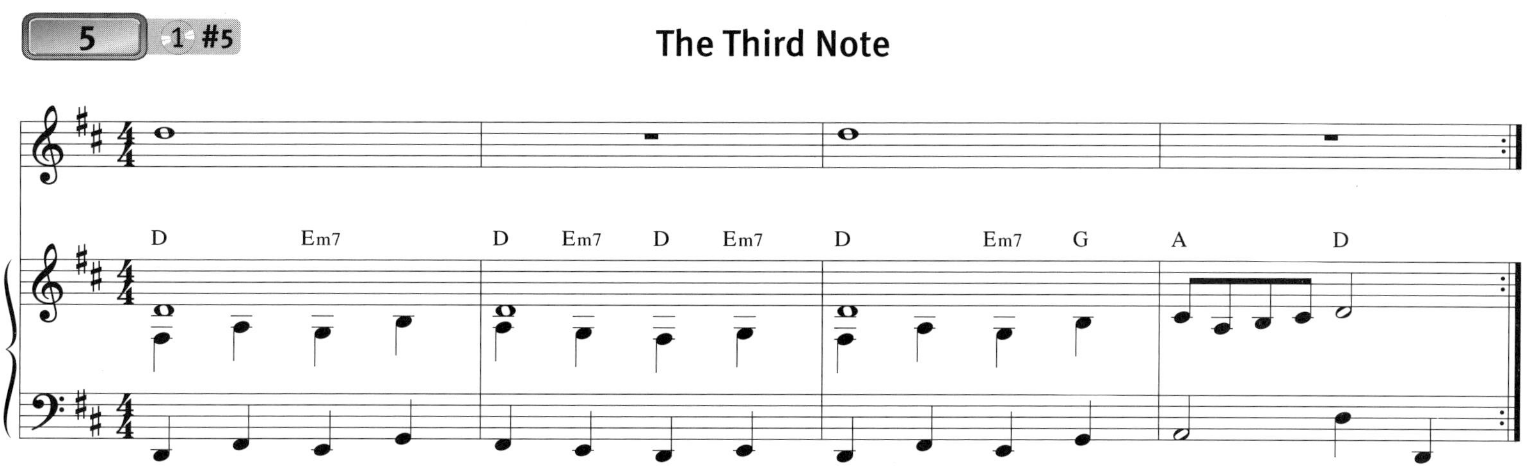

6 1 #6

It's Easy Now

7 1 #7

Triple Play

8
1 #8
Same Notes New Look
B♭ E♭ B♭/D Cm7 F7
B♭ E♭ B♭ B♭/D Cm F B♭
9
1 #9
More New Notation
F/B♭ E♭/B♭ B♭ F/B♭ E♭/B♭ B♭
F/A Gm7 Cm7 E♭/F B♭/F E♭/F B♭/F E♭/F B♭
10
1 #10
Listen While You Play
Woodwinds All Brass All Percussion All
N.C. B♭ F/A B♭ F/A Gm7 E♭/F F B♭

11
1 #11
Now You're Movin'
E♭ F/E♭ E♭ F/E♭ B♭/D E♭ F/E♭ E♭ B♭
E♭/G F/A B♭ B♭/F E♭/F B♭/F F7 B♭
12
1 #12
ADVANTAGE THEORY
B♭ E♭/B♭ F/A E♭/G B♭/F E♭/F F Gm7 F/A
B♭ E♭/B♭ F/A E♭/G B♭/F F7 B♭
13
1 #13
Duet Now
(Duet)
SANDY FELDSTEIN & LARRY CLARK
(b. 1940) (b. 1963)
1.
2.
B♭ E♭ B♭ B♭ E♭ B♭ B♭ E♭/B♭ B♭/F E♭/F B♭/F E♭/F B♭/F B♭

14
1 #14
New Note
Cm
Ab
Cm
Fm7 Bb/F Cm
Gm7Cm7Gm7
Cm
15
1 #15
New Note Exercise
Bb
F7
Bb
F7
Bb
16
1 #16
Another New Note
Bb
Gm
Bb
Eb
Bb
F7
Bb
F7
Bb
17
1 #17
New Note Workout
Bb
F7
Bb F7 Bb F
Bb
Cm7
F7
Bb
F7
Bb F7 Bb F
Bb F7 Bb
F7
Bb

18
1 #18
Hot Cross Buns
English Folk Song
B♭ F7 B♭ B♭ F7 B♭ F7 B♭ F7 B♭
19
1 #19
ADVANTAGE
PLAY BY EAR · Lightly Row
German Folk Song
B♭ F7 B♭ F7
B♭ F7 B♭ F7 B♭
20
1 #20
Rock Time
(Duet)
SANDY FELDSTEIN & LARRY CLARK
(b. 1940) (b. 1963)
1.
2.
B♭7 E♭7 B♭7 F7
B♭7 F7 B♭7 F7 B♭

21 1 #21

Good King Wenceslas

English Carol

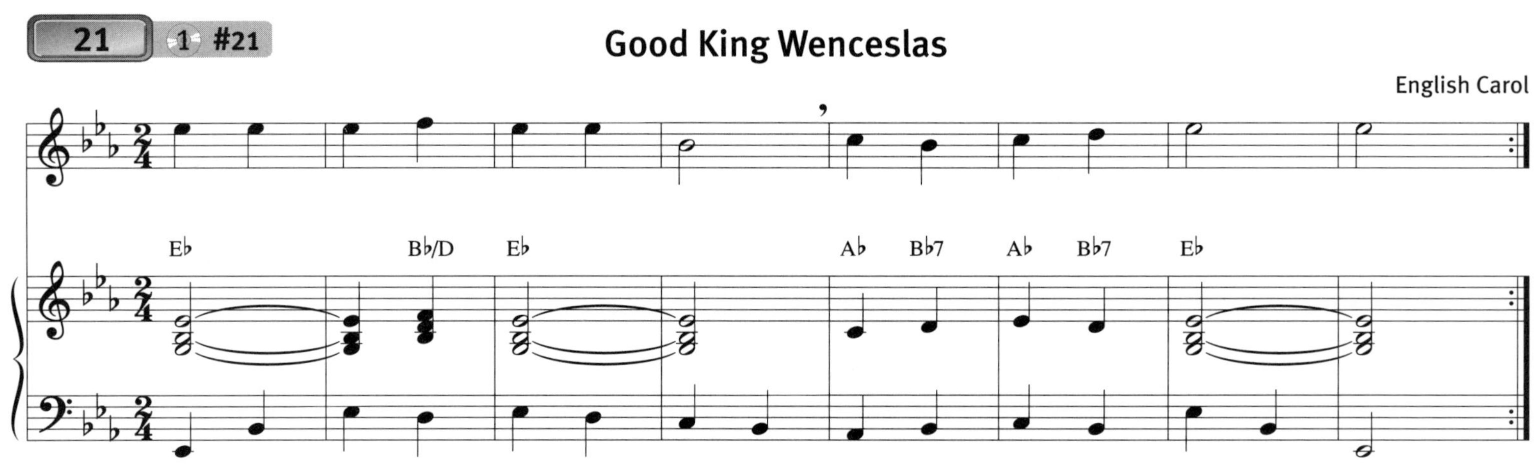

22 1 #22

Merrily We Roll Along

Traditional

23 1 #23

Jingle Bells

JAMES PEIRPONT
(1822–1893)

24
1 #24
Love Somebody
English Folk Song
Introduction
B♭ Cm7 B♭/D Cm7 B♭ C7 F7/A F B♭ F/A
Song
B♭ Gm7 Cm7 F7 B♭ Gm Cm7 F7 B♭ B♭7/A♭ E♭/G E♭m B♭/F F7 B♭
26
1 #26
Ode to Joy
(Duet)
LUDWIG van BEETHOVEN
(1770–1827)
1.
2.
B♭ Cm7 B♭/D F7 B♭ F/A Gm F/A B♭ F/A F
B♭ Cm7 B♭/D F7/C B♭ F/A Gm F/A B♭ F7 B♭

27 1 #27

New Note

28 1 #28

Tie Them Up

29 1 #29

Old MacDonald

Traditional

31 1 #31

Jolly Old St. Nicholas
(Duet)

Traditional Carol

ADVANTAGE 1 #94
FIRST CONCERT

The Victors
Chorale and March

Traditional
arranged by Sandy Feldstein & Larry Clark

ADVANTAGE 1 #95

FIRST CONCERT

When the Saints Go Marching In

Traditional
arranged by Sandy Feldstein & Larry Clark

32
1 #32
New Note
F Bb/D F Bb/D Bb F Gm7 F/A Bb F F7
Bb/D Eb Bb/D Bb Bb F/A Gm7 F Bb/D F/C Bb
33
1 #33
A Half Step at a Time
f p
Bb F/Bb Bb F/Bb Eb/Bb Bb Eb/Bb Bb Eb/Bb Bb F Gm7 F/A F
f p f
Bb F/Bb Eb/Bb F Bb Bb/D Bb Eb Bb F/A F Bb
34
1 #34
Scale Study
f
Bb F/A Bb Eb Bb Eb Bb/D Cm7 Bb F/A Bb/F F Bb

35
#35
Shoo Fly
American Folk Song
Fast
36
#36
ADVANTAGE
MUSICIANSHIP (DYNAMICS)
37
#37
Russian Folk Song
(Duet)
LUDWIG van BEETHOVEN
(1770–1827)
Moderately

38
1 #38
Chorale Warm-up
(Three-part Round)
A. Slow
B.
p
f
Bb F/A Bb Eb/G Bb Bb/F F/A Bb Eb/G Bb/D Eb
C.
Bb/D Cm7 Bb Bb/D Eb Cm7 Bb Gm F N.C. Bb/D Cm7 Bb
39
1 #39
Klosé Technique Study
HYACINTHE-ELÉONORE KLOSÉ
(1808–80)
Bb F/C Bb/D Bb Bb/D F/C Bb Cm G/D Cm/Eb Cm Cm/Eb G/D Cm
Bb Cm7 Bb/D Bb Bb/D Cm7 Bb Cm7 Bb/D Cm7 Bb/D Fsus F7 Bb
40
1 #40
Cassions Song
EDMUND L. GRUBER
(1879–1941)
Fast
Bb F7 Bb

41
1 #41
Mary Ann
Moderately
Jamaican Folk Song
B♭
F
B♭
N.C.
B♭
F
B♭
B♭/F F
B♭
42
1 #42
ADVANTAGE
PLAY BY EAR · London Bridge
Moderately
English Folk Song
B♭
Cm7
B♭ Cm7 B♭/D
F
F7
B♭ Cm7 B♭/D
B♭
Cm7
B♭ Cm7 B♭/D
F
B♭
43
1 #43
Ha'kyo Jung
The School Bell Is Ringing
(Duet)
Moderately
Korean Folk Song
1.
2.
B♭
Cm7/B♭
B♭
F7
B♭
Cm7/B♭
B♭
F
B♭

44 1 #44

Chorale Warm-up

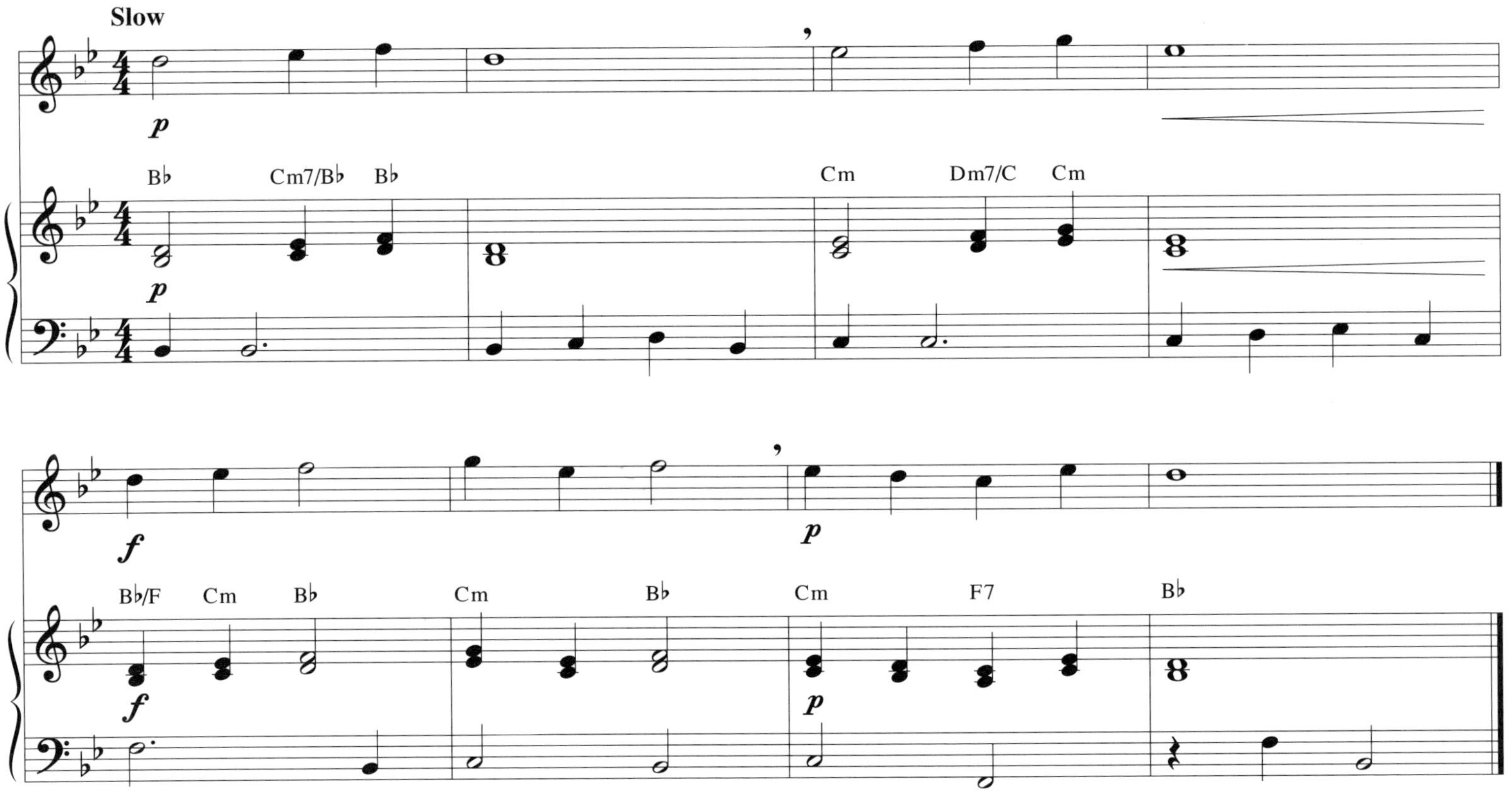

Slow
p
B♭ Cm7/B♭ B♭ Cm Dm7/C Cm
p
f
p
B♭/F Cm B♭ Cm B♭ Cm F7 B♭
f
p

45 1 #45

Eighth-Note Study

f
B♭ F F7/A B♭ F B♭
f

46 1 #46

Two in a Row

p
f
E♭ B♭/D E♭ B♭ Cm B♭ A♭ B♭7 E♭
p
f

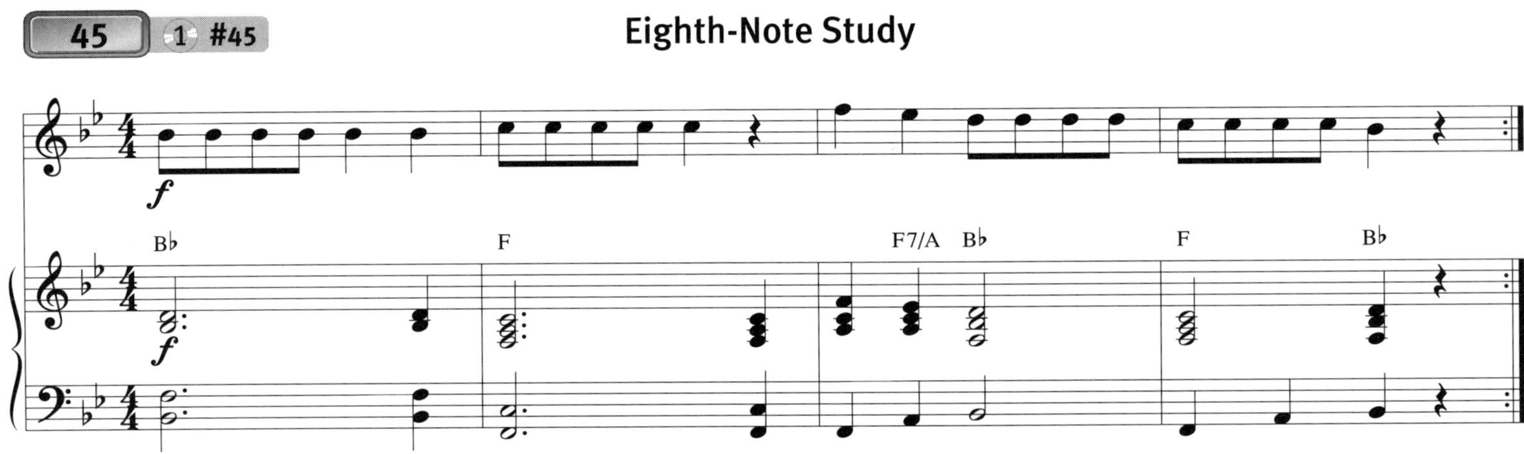

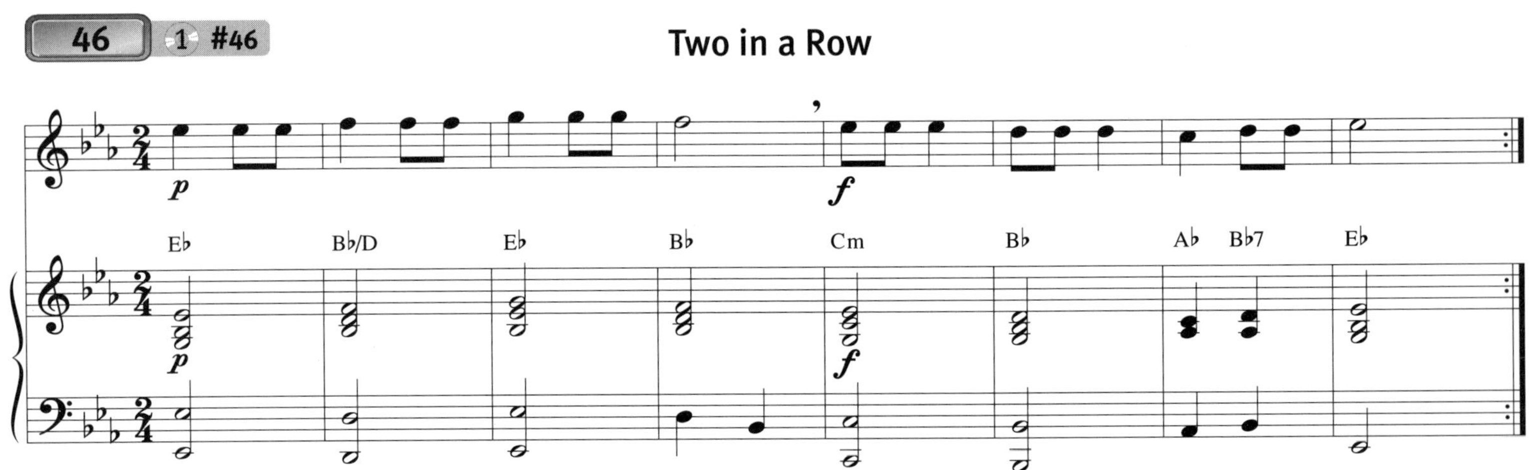

47 ① #47

Baa Baa Black Sheep

American Folk Song

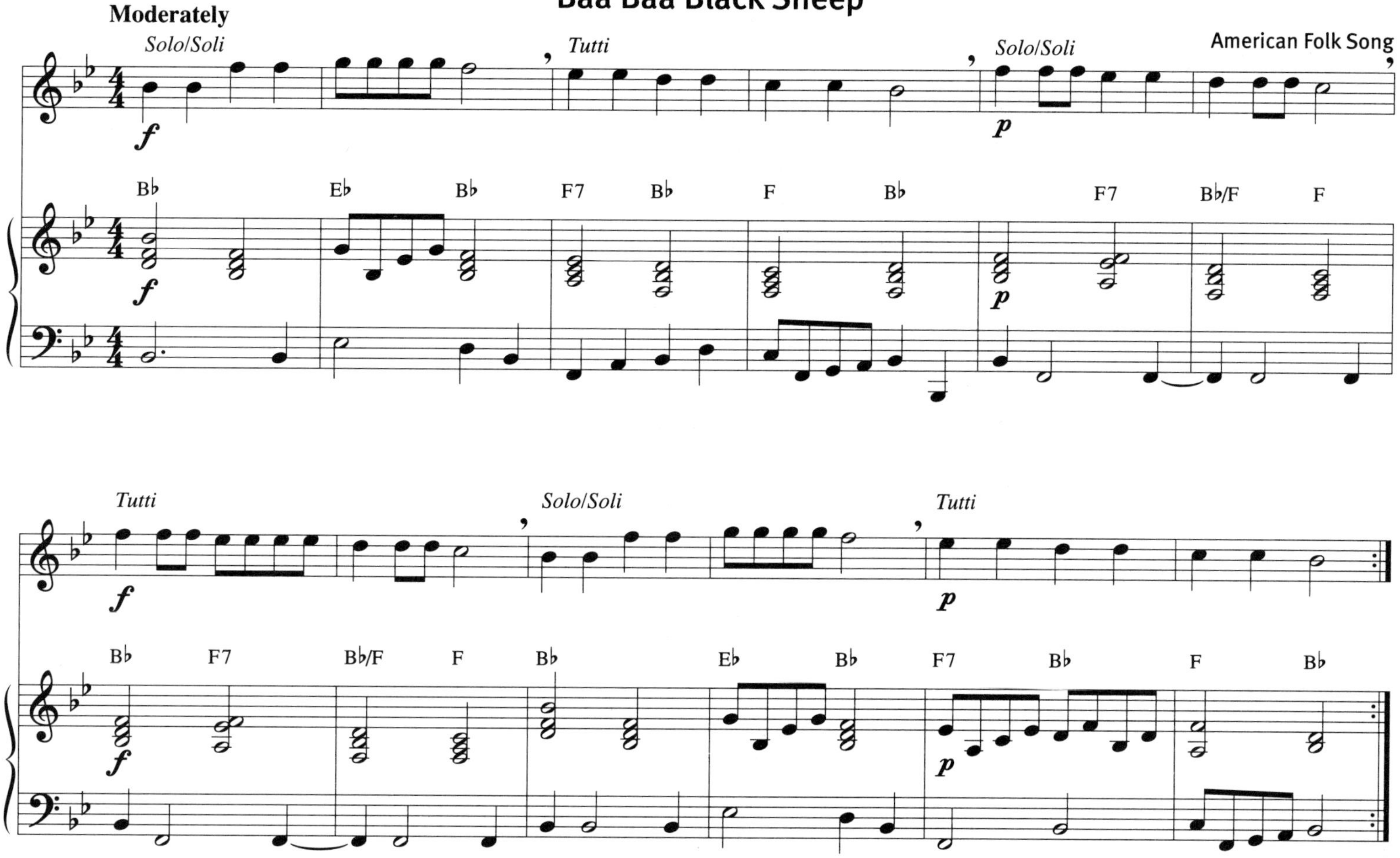

Moderately

Solo/Soli *f* — *Tutti* — *Solo/Soli* *p*

B♭ E♭ B♭ F7 B♭ F B♭ F7 B♭/F F

Tutti *f* — *Solo/Soli* — *Tutti* *p*

B♭ F7 B♭/F F B♭ E♭ B♭ F7 B♭ F B♭

49 ① #49

Skip to My Lou
(Duet)

American Folk Song

50
1 #50
New Note
C F C F C/E Dm7 C F/A C/B♭ F/A C7 F
51
1 #51
New Note Exercise
F C7/G F/A Gm/B♭ Dm Am/C B♭ F/A B♭ C7/B♭ F/A C7 F C/F F
52
1 #52
Scale Study
F C7/G Am Gm F Gm F B♭ C F Gm7 F/A C7/B♭
F Gm7 F/A F B♭/C C7 B♭/C C7 F
53
1 #53
Aura Lee Rocks
Rock Tempo
Theme
American Folk Song
F G7 Gm7/C F Gm7 F

F
G7
Gm7/C
F Gm7 F
Variation
G7
Gm7/C
F Gm7 F
G7
Gm7/C
F Gm7 F
55
1 #55
Frère Jacques
(Round)
French Folk Song
A.
Moderately
B.
B♭ F/C B♭
B♭ F/C B♭
Cm7 B♭/D
B♭ Cm7 B♭/D
C.
D.
B♭

56 Chorale Warm-up

57 Scale Study

58 Barcarolle

JACQUES OFFENBACH (1819–1880)

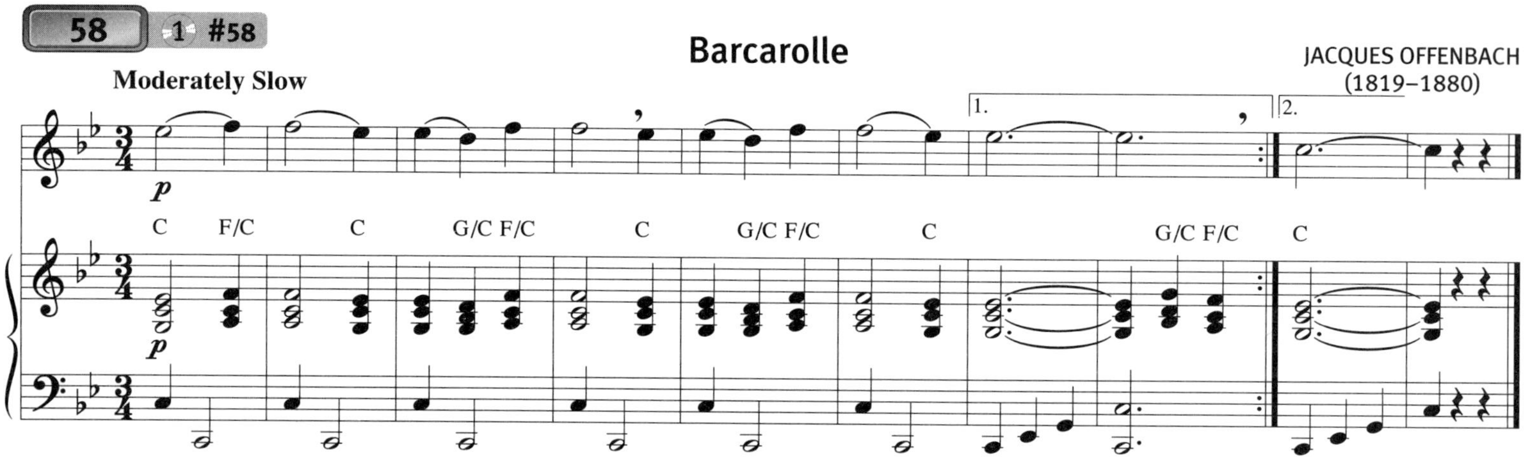

59 This Old Man

American Folk Song

Bb/D
Gm7
Bb/F
F
F7
Bb
60
1 #60
ADVANTAGE
THEORY
F
C
Bb/D C/E Bb/F
F
C/E Bb/D
C7
F
C7
F
61
1 #61
Blue Danube Waltz
(Duet)
JOHANN STRAUSS
(1804–1849)
Fast
1.
2.
N.C.
Bb
F7
1a.
2a.
Bb
Eb7
F9
Bb

62 1 #62

Long Tone Warm-up

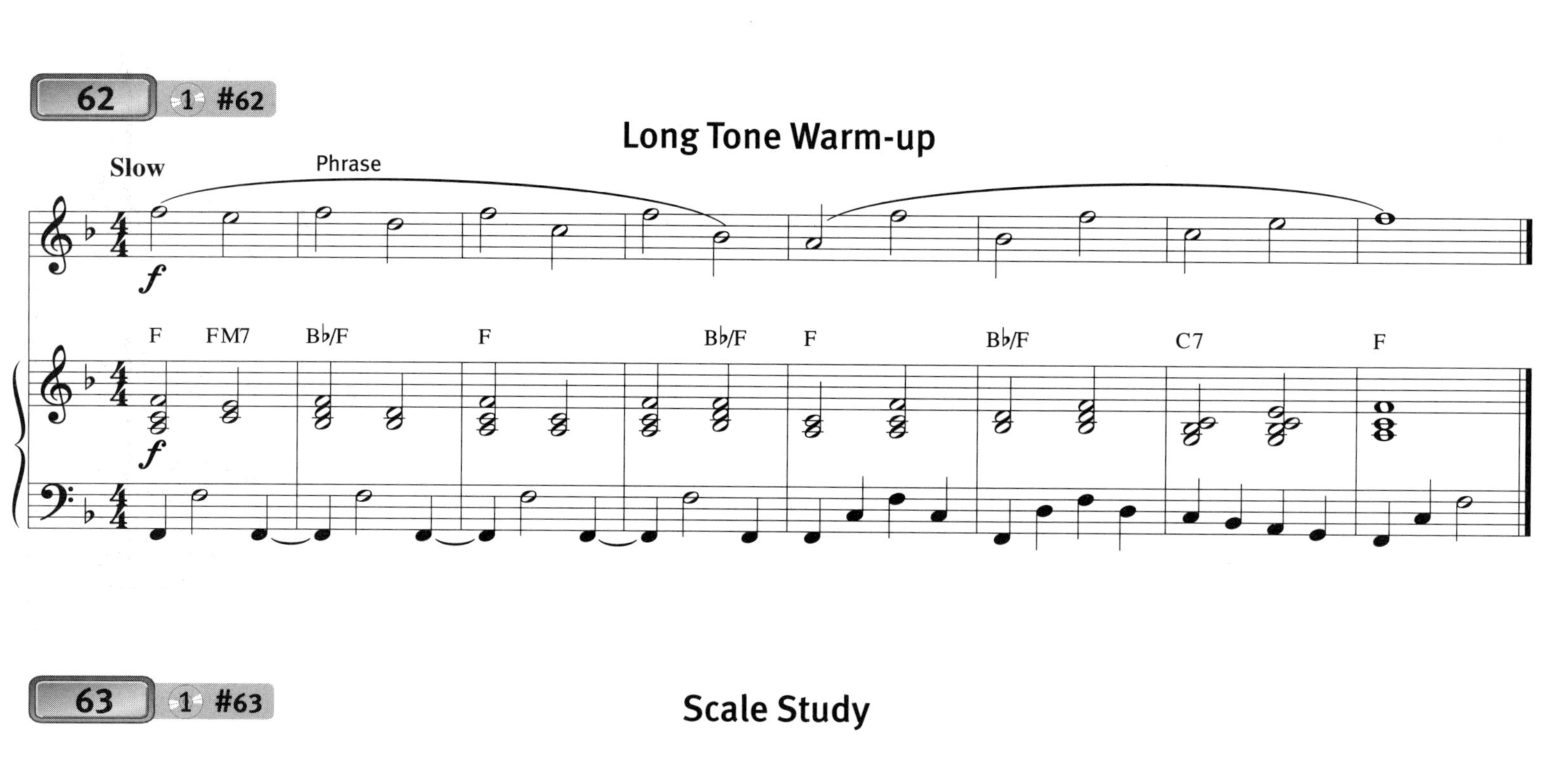

Slow
Phrase
f
F FM7 B♭/F F B♭/F F B♭/F C7 F
f

63 1 #63

Scale Study

f
F B♭ F B♭ C F F/A F B♭ F C7 F
f

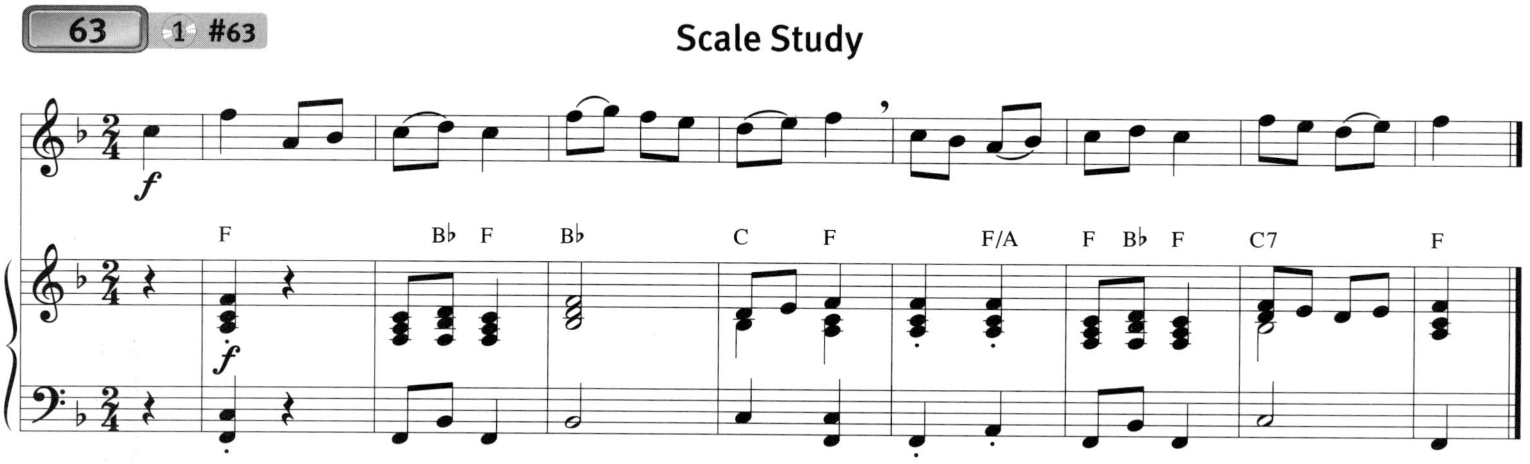

64 1 #64

Symphony No. 1
(Theme)

JOHANNES BRAHMS
(1833–97)

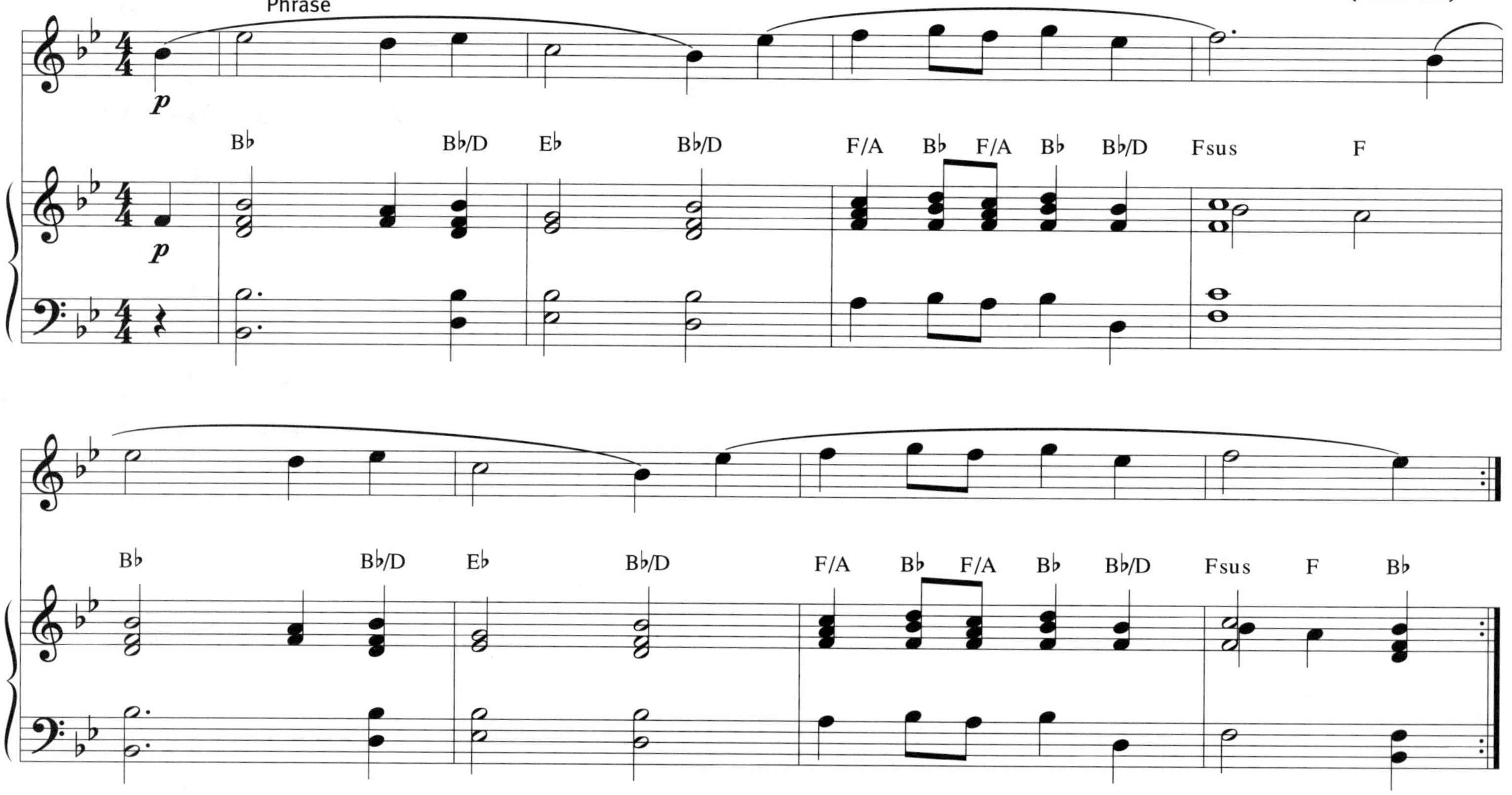

Moderately Slow
Phrase
p
B♭ B♭/D E♭ B♭/D F/A B♭ F/A B♭ B♭/D Fsus F
p
B♭ B♭/D E♭ B♭/D F/A B♭ F/A B♭ B♭/D Fsus F B♭

65
1 #65
Mexican Hat Dance
Mexican Folk Song
Fast
Bb F7 F9 F7 Bb Gm7/Bb
F7 F9 F7 Bb F7 Bb
67
1 #67
Academic Festival Overture
(Duet)
JOHANNES BRAHMS
(1833–97)
Fast
Bb F Bb Eb/G Bb/D Eb
Bb Cm7 Bb Bb/D Bb F/A F Bb F Bb

68 1 #68

Chorale Warm-up

69 1 #69

Clarke Technique Study

HERBERT L. CLARKE
(1867–1945)

70 1 #70

Musette

JOHANN SEBASTIAN BACH
(1685–1750)

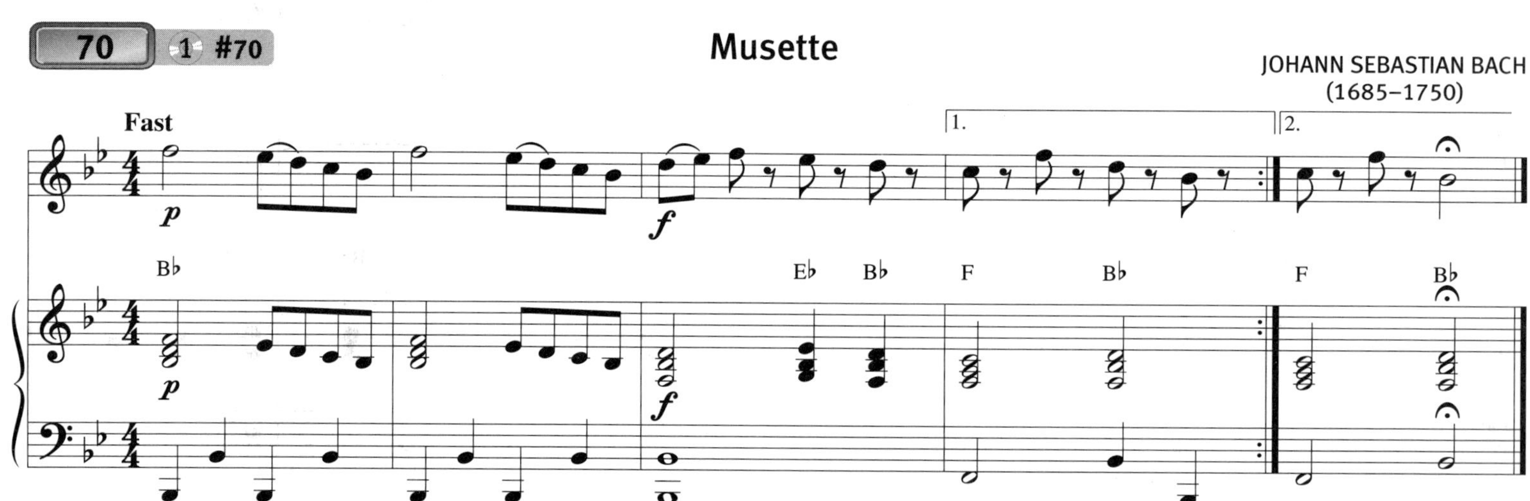

71 1 #71

Old St. Nick in Eighths

Traditional

73 1 #73

Lovely Evening
(Round)

French Folk Song

A. Moderately

p

B♭ F B♭ E♭ B♭ B♭/D Cm7 B♭ E♭ B♭ B♭/D Cm7 B♭

p

B.

B♭ F B♭ E♭ B♭ B♭/D Cm7 B♭ E♭ B♭ B♭/D Cm7 B♭

C.

B♭ F B♭ E♭ B♭ B♭/D Cm7 B♭ E♭ B♭ B♭/D Cm7 B♭

ADVANTAGE PERFORMANCE
1 #96
Carnival of Venice
Theme and Variation
Italian Folk Song
arranged by Sandy Feldstein & Larry Clark
Introduction
Fast
Theme
Bb Eb/G Bb/D Cm Em7(b5) F Bb6 Cm/Bb F7 C F9/A F9 Eb/Bb F7 Eb Bb/F

ADVANTAGE
PERFORMANCE
1 #97
Conquest
SANDY FELDSTEIN & LARRY CLARK
(b. 1940) (b. 1963)
Fast

74 1 #74
New Note Warm-up
Eb Bb Eb Ab Bb Eb/Bb Ab/Bb Eb
Ab/Eb Eb Ab/Eb Bb/D Eb Bb7/F Eb/G Fm7 Eb/G Fm/Ab Bb7 Eb
75 1 #75
Scale Study
Eb Fm7 Bb9 Eb Bb Cm7 Bb/D Eb N.C. Eb
76 1 #76
12 Bar Blues
Moderately
Bb Eb/Bb Bb9 Bb7 Bb Bb7 Eb7
Bb F7 Eb7 Bb7

77 1 #77

Merry Widow Waltz

FRANZ LEHÁR
(1870–1948)

79 1 #79

Lo Yisa Goy
(Round)

Israeli Folk Song

A. Moderately Slow

p

Cm B♭ Gm Cm B♭ Gm Cm

p

B.

1. 2.

B♭ Gm Cm Cm G7 Cm

80 1 #80

Listening Skills Warm-up

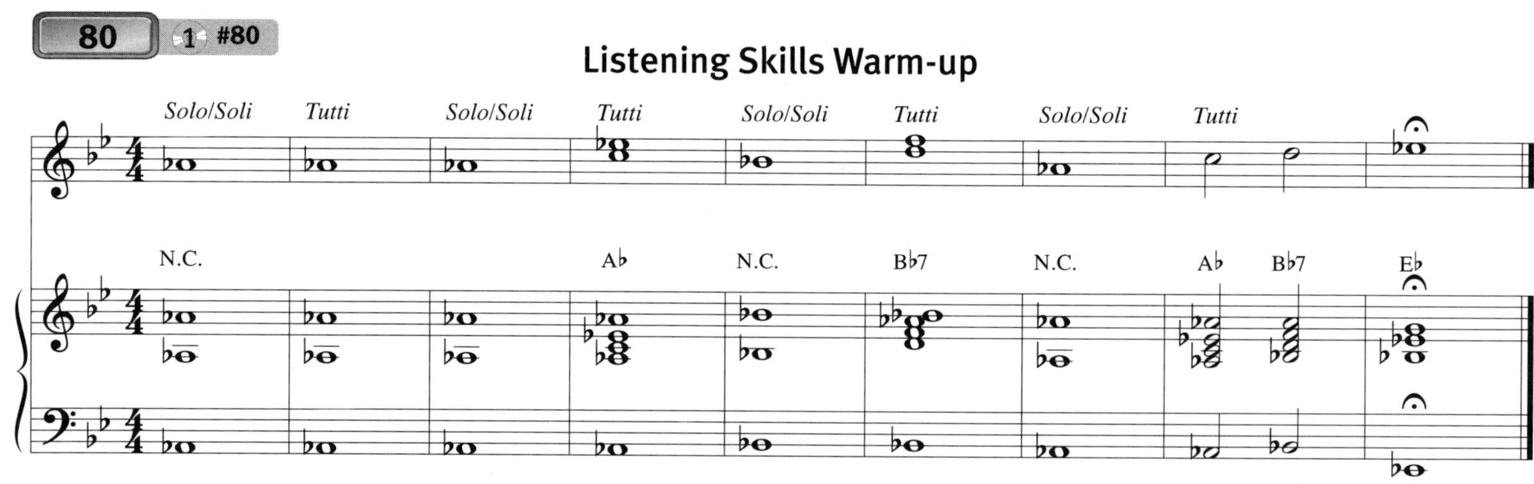

81 1 #81

Tongue Twister

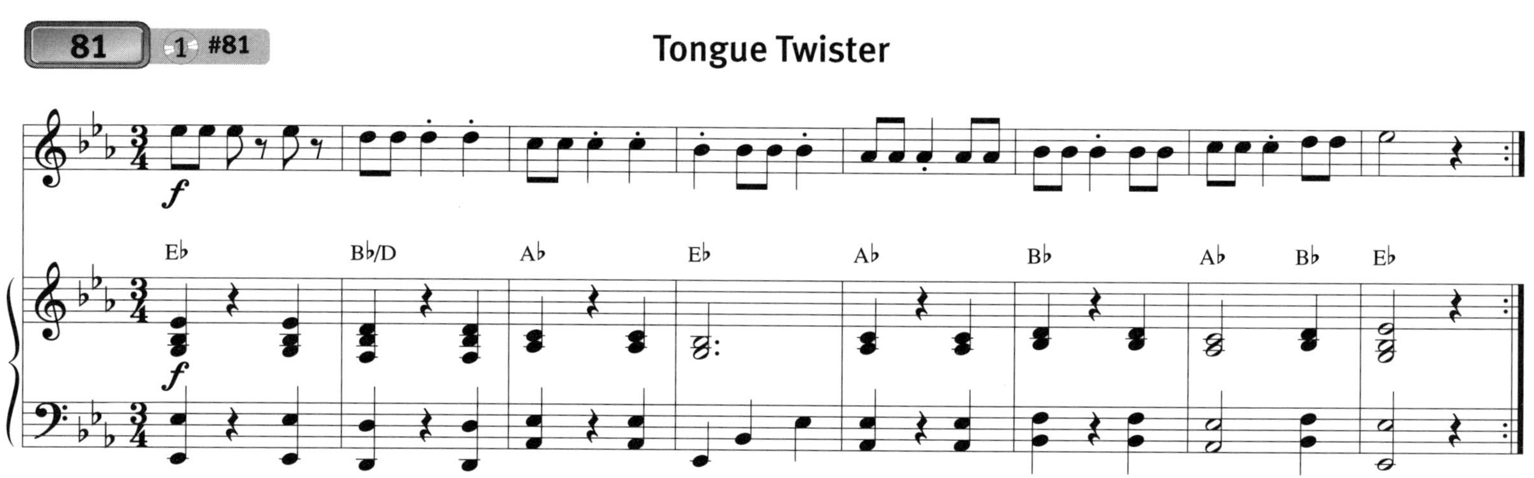

82 1 #82

Camptown Races

STEPHEN FOSTER
(1826–1864)

83 1 #83

Spring Theme
from *The Four Seasons*

ANTONIO VIVALDI
(1678–1741)

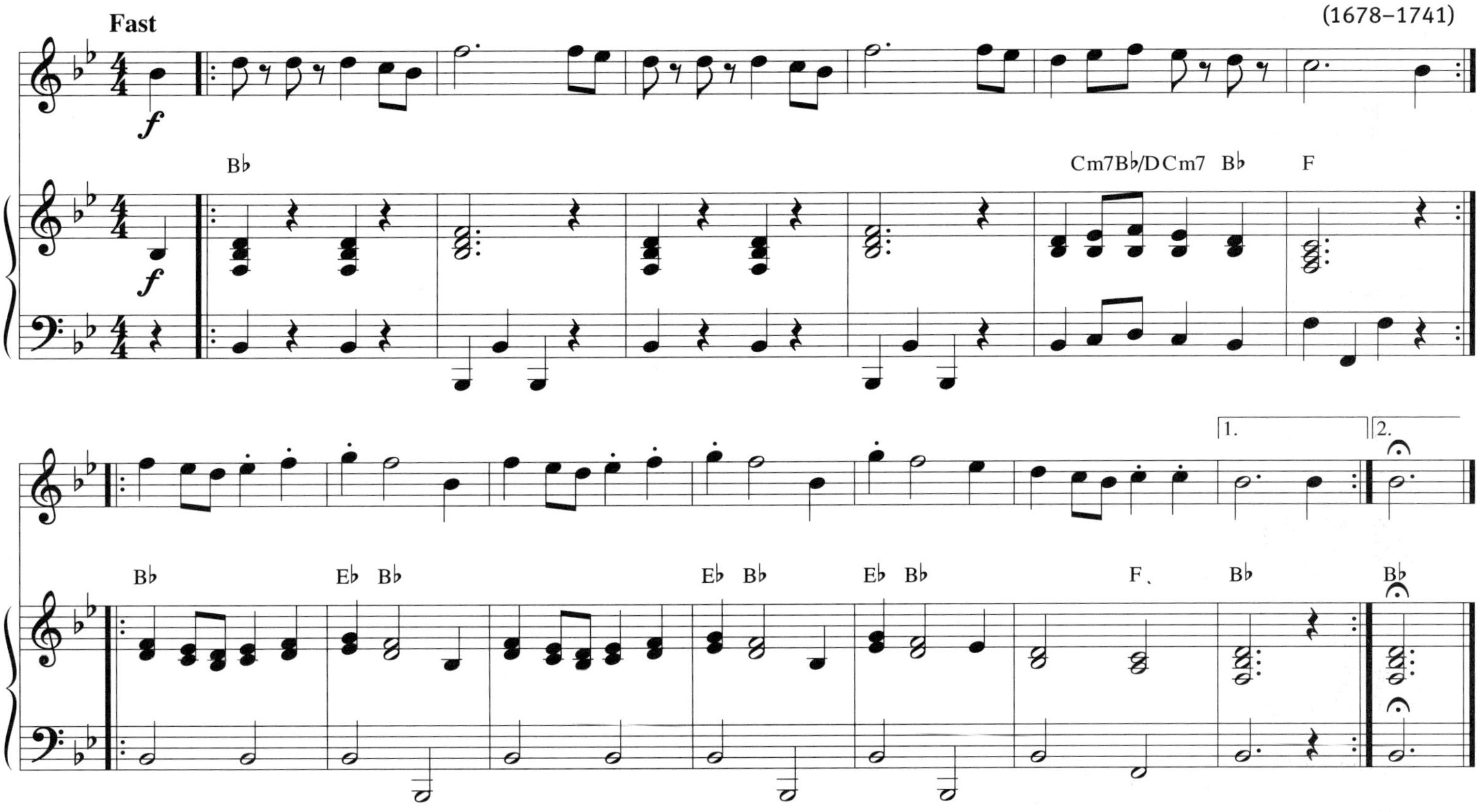

Fast
f
B♭
Cm7 B♭/D Cm7 B♭
F
f
1.
2.
B♭
E♭ B♭
E♭ B♭
E♭ B♭
F
B♭
B♭

85 1 #85

Écossaise
(Duet)

LUDWIG van BEETHOVEN
(1770–1827)

1.
Fast
p
f
2.
p
f
A♭
E♭/G
Fm
A♭/E♭
E♭
A♭
E♭/G
E♭
A♭
p
f
1.
2.

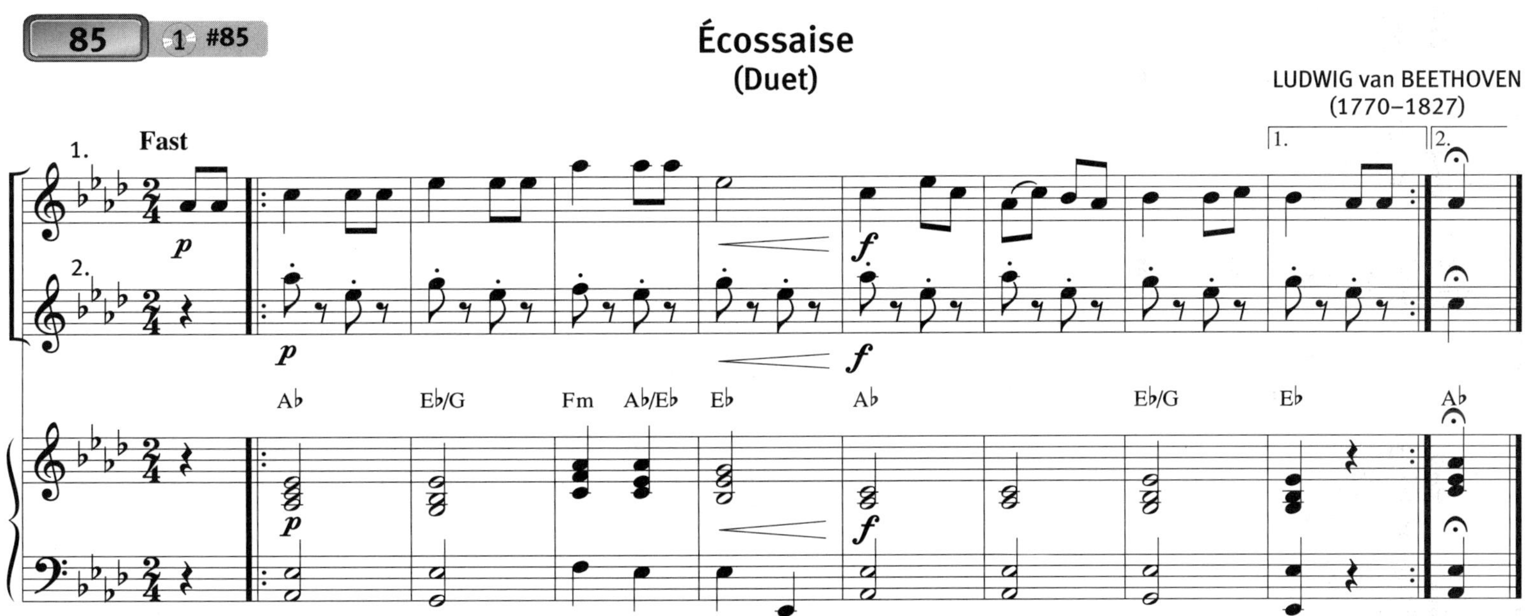

86 1 #86
Scaling Up Warm-up
B♭ E♭ F Gm Dm/F Gm F E♭ F B♭/D F E♭ B♭/D Cm7 B♭ F B♭
87 1 #87
New Note Exercise
F Gm7 F/A B♭ Gm F/A Gm/B♭ B° C7 B♭7 F Gm7 F/A B♭ C B♭/D F/A Gm7 F C7 F
88 1 #88
New Rhythm
F C/E F C/E F C/E F C/E F C/E F B♭/F F C/E F C/E F/C F
89 1 #89
Lullaby
JOHANNES BRAHMS
(1833–97)
Andante
B♭ F7 B♭

90 1 #90
Inkpataya
Native American Folk Song
Allegro
Gm Bb Fm Gm7 Fm/Ab N.C. Cm Fm N.C.
91 1 #91
Chorale St. Anthony
FRANZ JOSEPH HAYDN
(1732–1809)
Andante
Eb Ab/EbEb Ab/Eb Eb Bb G7/BCm7 Fm7/Ab Am7b5 Eb/Bb Bb Fm7/Ab Eb/BbBb Bb7 Eb
92 1 #92
ADVANTAGE
PLAY BY EAR · Twinkle Twinkle
Bb Eb/B Bb Eb Bb F Bb Eb Bb F Bb Eb Bb F7 Bb Eb/BbBb Eb Bb F7 Bb
93 1 #93
Trumpet Voluntary
(Duet)
JEREMIAH CLARKE
(1674–1707)
Andante
F C/E F Bb F C/E F C/G F/A C/GF/A C F Gm7 F Gm7 F

94 2 #1
B♭ Scale and Chord Progression
f
B♭ F B♭ Cm7 F7 E♭/G F7/A B♭ F/A E♭/G B♭/F E♭ B♭ F B♭ E♭ B♭ F7 B♭
95 2 #2
Surprise Symphony
(Theme)
FRANZ JOSEPH HAYDN
(1732–1809)
Moderato
p
f
B♭ B♭/D F7 B♭ B♭/D C7 F
F7 B♭/F F7 B♭ B♭/D F7 B♭
96 2 #3
Morning
from Peer Gynt Suite No. 1
EDVARD GRIEG
(1843–1907)
Andante
p
A♭(9) A♭ A♭(9) A♭ Fm A♭
97 2 #4
Can-Can
from Orpheus in the Underworld
JACQUES OFFENBACH
(1819–80)
Allegro
f
B♭ F7 B♭ F7 B♭ F7

1.
2.
Bb F7 Bb F7 Bb F7 Bb Bb
98 2 #5
ADVANTAGE MUSICIANSHIP
Eb/G Bb/D Eb Bb/D Eb Ab/C Eb Bb/D Cm7 Bb Cm7 Bb/D Bb
Eb/G Bb/D Eb Bb/D Ab Bb7 Eb Bb Eb
99 2 #6
Kookabura
(Round)
Australian Folk Song
A.
Moderato
B.
C.
D.
Bb Eb/Bb Bb Bb Eb/Bb Bb
Bb Eb/Bb Bb Eb/Bb Bb

100 2 #7
Pachelbel Canon Chorale
JOHANN PACHELBEL
(1653–1706)
Andante
B♭ Fsus F Gm9-8 Dm E♭ B♭ E♭ F7 B♭
101 2 #8
E♭ Scale and Chord Progression
E♭ B♭/D E♭ A♭ B♭7 A♭/C B♭7/D E♭ B♭/D A♭/C B♭7 Gm/B♭ B♭ E♭ A♭ E♭ B♭7 E♭
102 2 #9
Swan Lake
(Theme)
PETER ILYICH TCHAIKOVSKY
(1840–93)
Andante
Cm Fm Cm A♭ Cm Cm
103 2 #10
William Tell Overture
(Theme)
GIOACHINO ROSSINI
(1792–1868)
Allegro
E♭ B♭ B♭7

E♭
B♭7
E♭
E♭
1.
2.
104
2 #11
ADVANTAGE
COMPOSITION/IMPROVISATION
B♭(9)
Cm7/B♭
E♭
B♭(9)
F/A
E♭/G
B♭/F
F
B♭
105
2 #12
Rockin' Riffs
(Ensemble)
SANDY FELDSTEIN & LARRY CLARK
(b. 1940)
(b. 1963)
Allegro
1.
2.
3.
f
F7
E♭7
F7
B♭7
F7
E♭7
F7
F7
B♭7
E♭7
F7

106 2 #13

Scaling Down

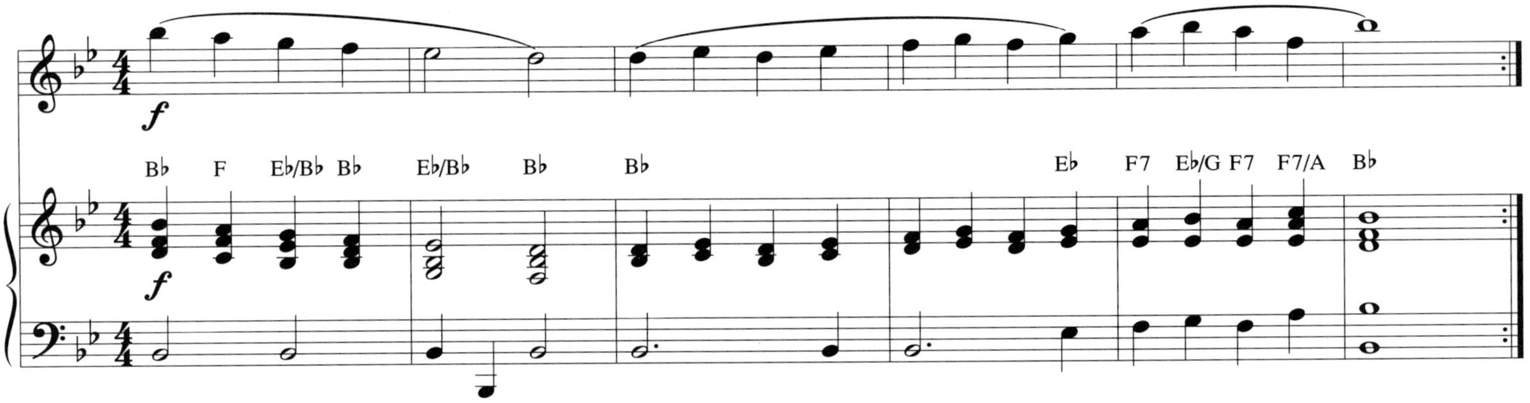

f

Bb F Eb/Bb Bb Eb/Bb Bb Bb Eb F7 Eb/G F7 F7/A Bb

107 2 #14

New Rhythm

f

Eb Cm Ab Bb Eb Bb Eb Ab/Eb Eb Bb/D Bb Eb

108 2 #15

F Scale and Chord Progression

Andante

p *f* *p* *f*

F Gm7 F/A Gm7 F/A Bb C7 Dm C7 Bb7 N.C. F Bb F C7 F

109 2 #16

Suo-Gan

Welsh Folk Song

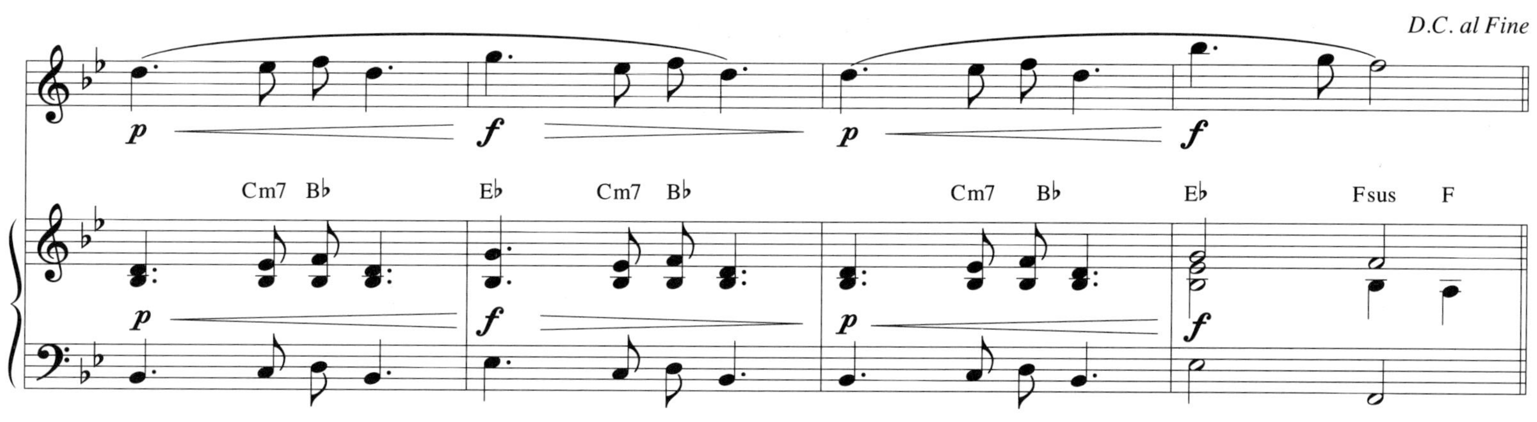

110 2 #17

Volga Boatman

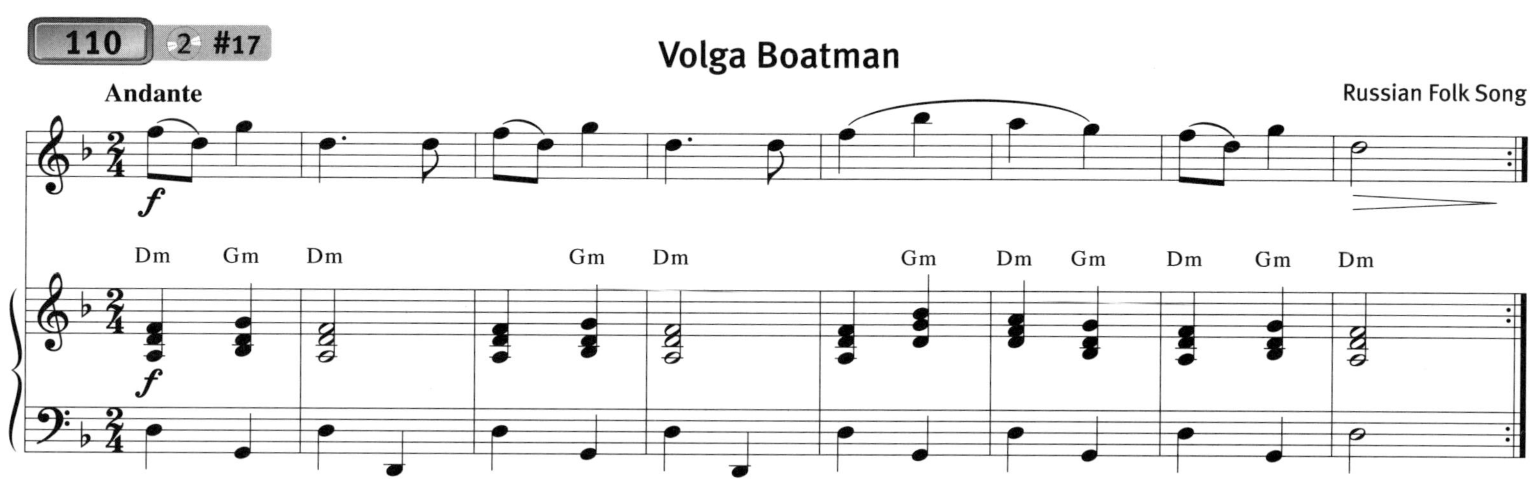

112 2 #19

Where Is John?
(Round)

American Folk Song

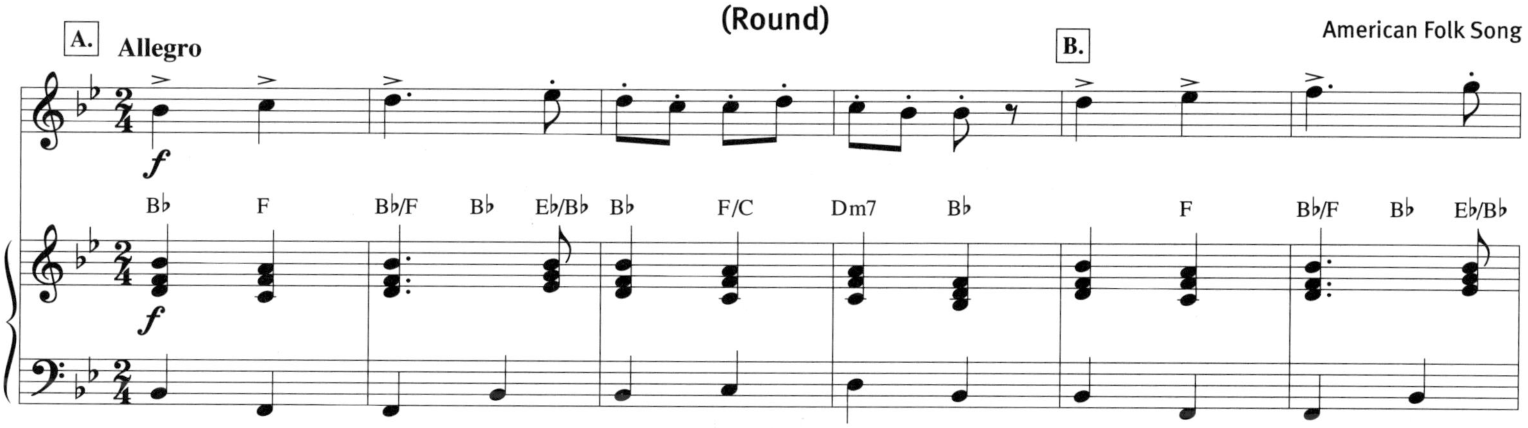

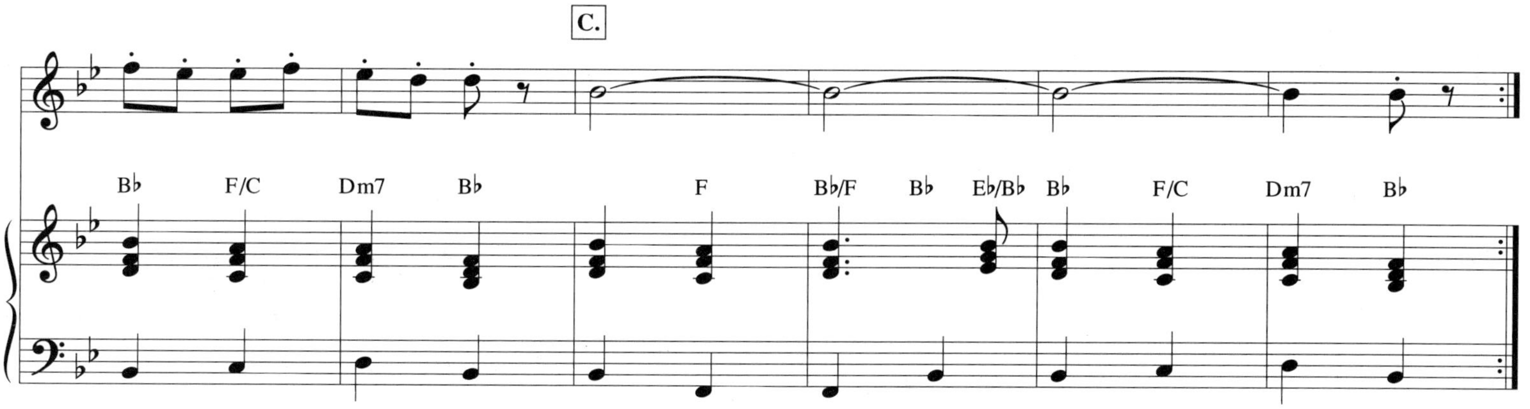

A. Allegro

B.

f

B♭ F B♭/F B♭ E♭/B♭ B♭ F/C Dm7 B♭ F B♭/F B♭ E♭/B♭

C.

B♭ F/C Dm7 B♭ F B♭/F B♭ E♭/B♭ B♭ F/C Dm7 B♭

113 (2) #20

Flexibility Warm-up

114 (2) #21

Home on the Range

American Folk Song

Andante

E♭ A♭ A♭m E♭ F7 Fm7/B♭ B♭ Cm7 B♭/D

Fine

E♭ A♭ A♭m E♭ B♭ Cm7 B♭/D E♭

D.S. al Fine

B♭9 E♭ B♭/D Cm7 F7 Fm7/B♭ B♭ Cm7 B♭/D

115 2 #22

Alouette

French-Canadian Folk Song

116 2 #23

Stone-Passing Game

African Folk Song

118 2 #25

We Wish You a Merry Christmas
(Duet)

Traditional

ADVANTAGE PERFORMANCE 2 #76

Shaker Settings

Father James's Song - JAMES WHITTAKER (1751–87)
Simple Gifts - JOSEPH BRACKETT (1797–1882)
arranged by Sandy Feldstein & Larry Clark

ADVANTAGE 2 #77
PERFORMANCE

Sousapalooza

JOHN PHILIP SOUSA
(1854–1932)
arranged by Sandy Feldstein & Larry Clark

119 2 #26

To the Next Level

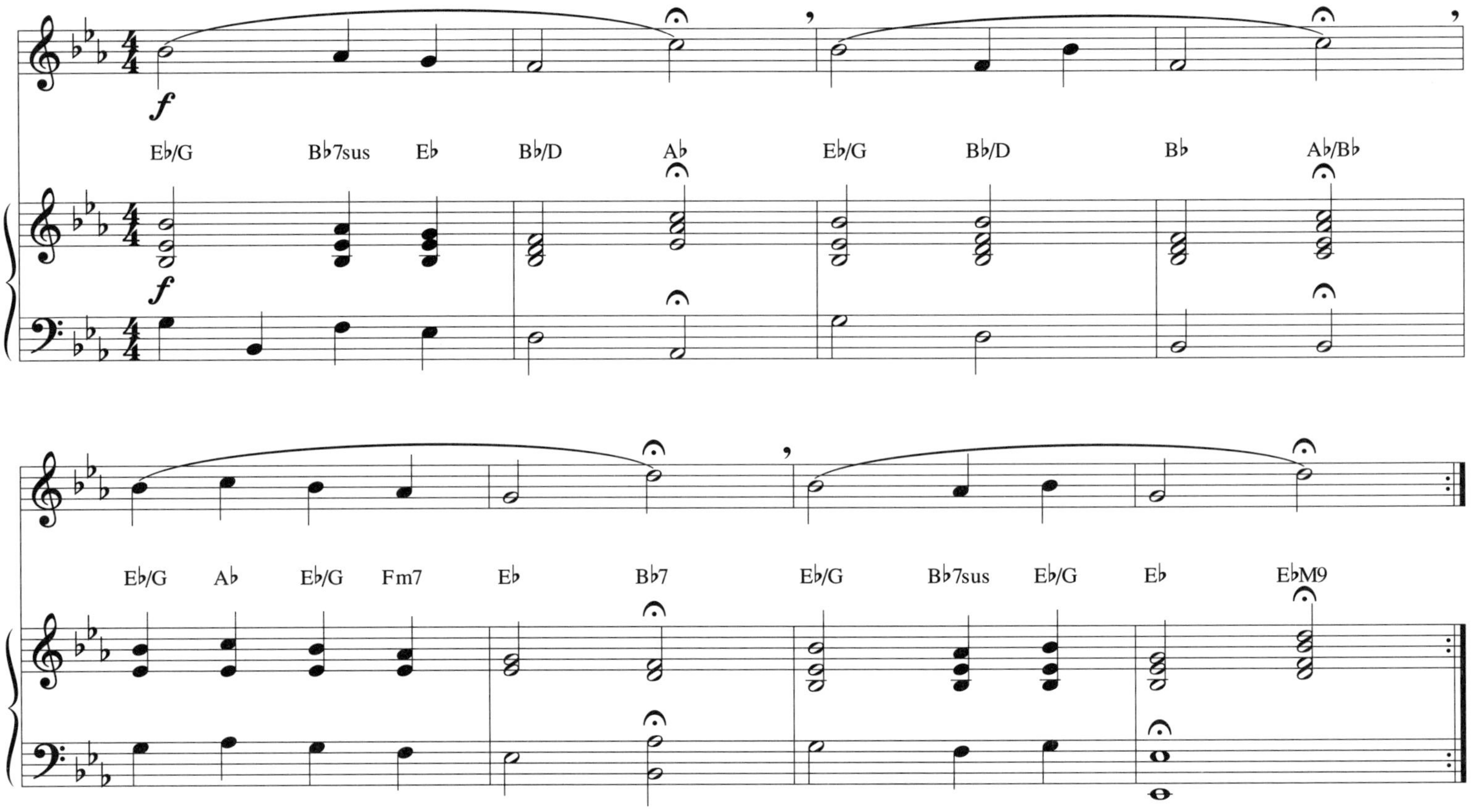

f

Eb/G Bb7sus Eb Bb/D Ab Eb/G Bb/D Bb Ab/Bb

f

Eb/G Ab Eb/G Fm7 Eb Bb7 Eb/G Bb7sus Eb/G Eb EbM9

120 2 #27

Above from Below

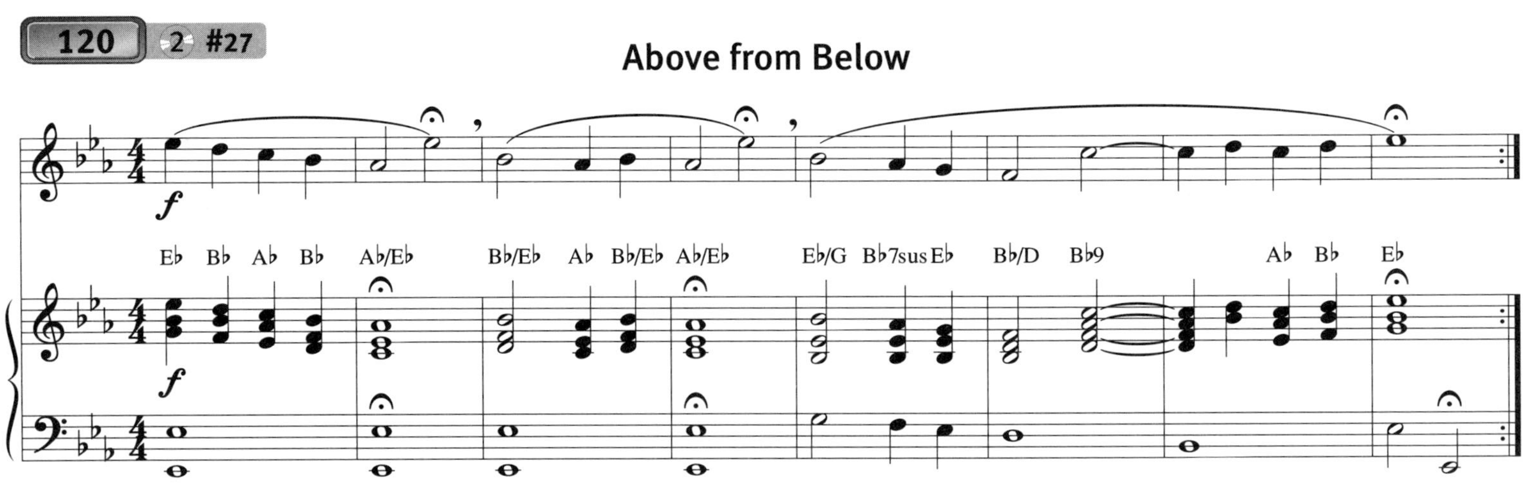

121 2 #28

Arban Scale Study

JEAN-BAPTISTE ARBAN
(1825–89)

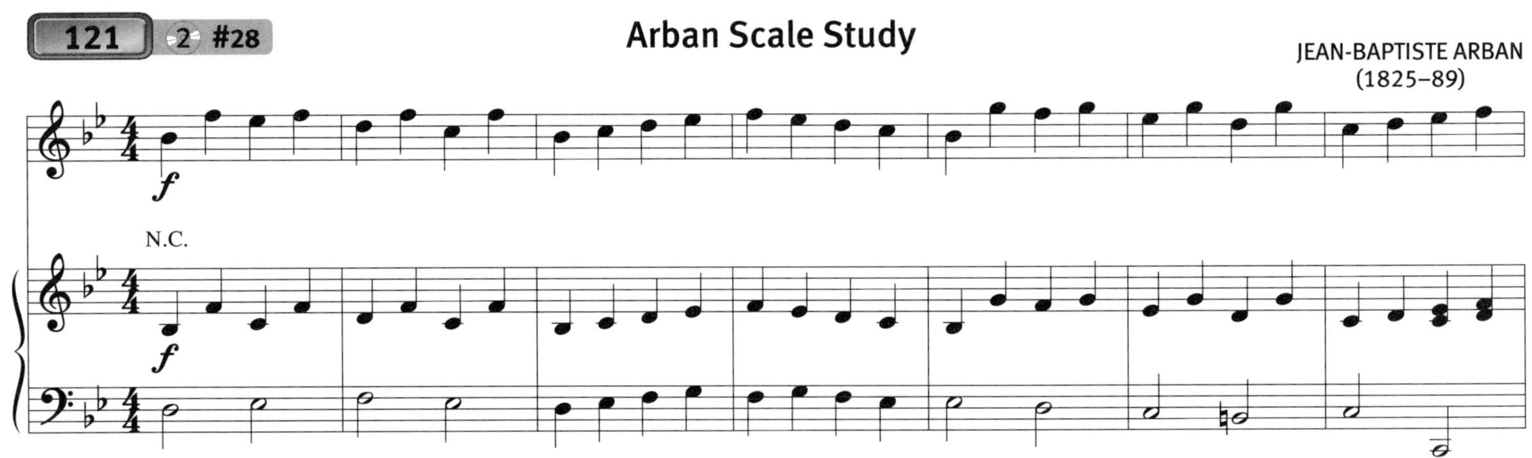

122 2 #29

Shepherd's Hey

English Folk Song

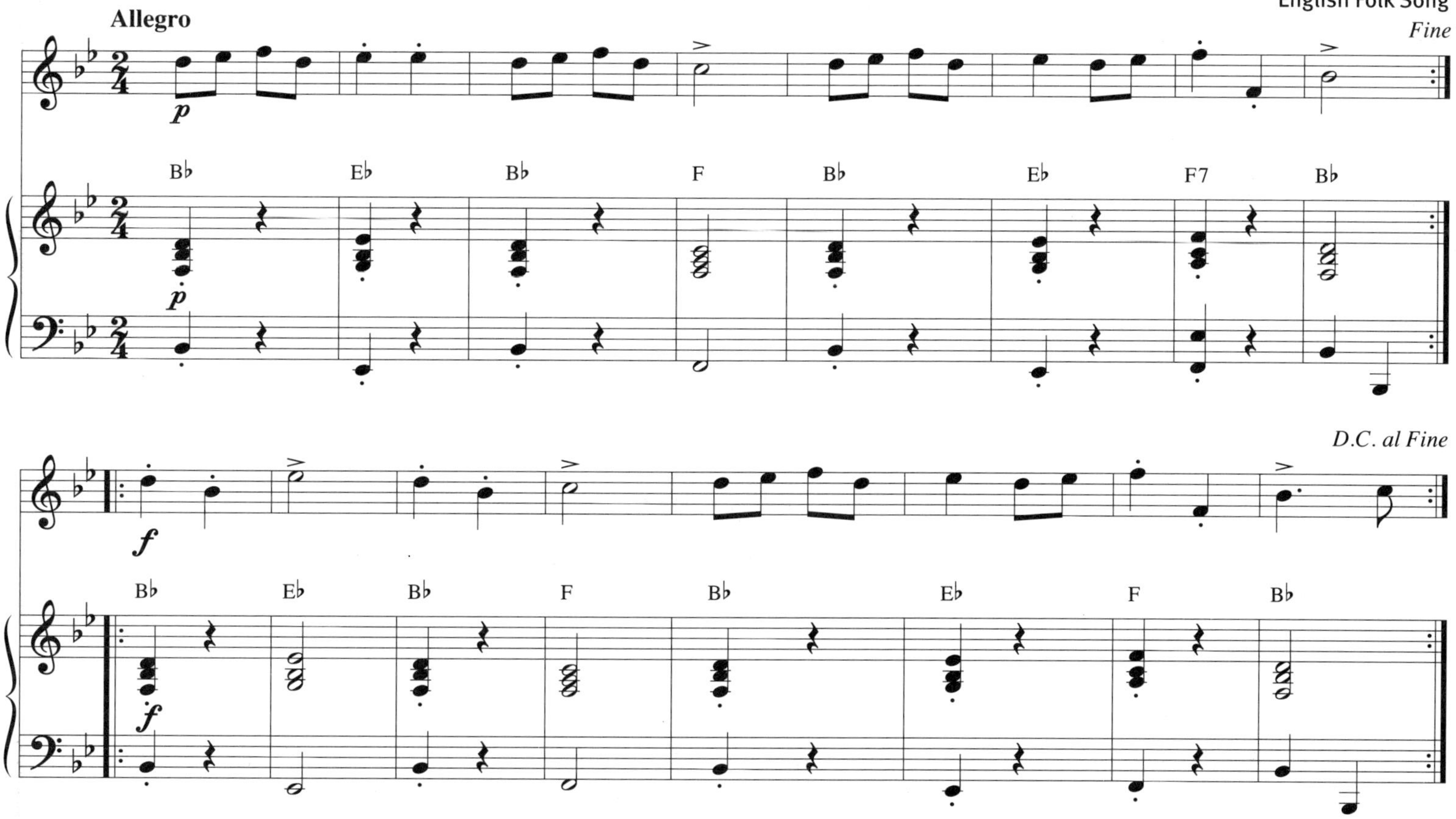

Allegro

p

Fine

B♭ E♭ B♭ F B♭ E♭ F7 B♭

p

D.C. al Fine

f

B♭ E♭ B♭ F B♭ E♭ F B♭

f

124 2 #31

Andantino
(Duet)

FRANZ SCHUBERT
(1797–1828)

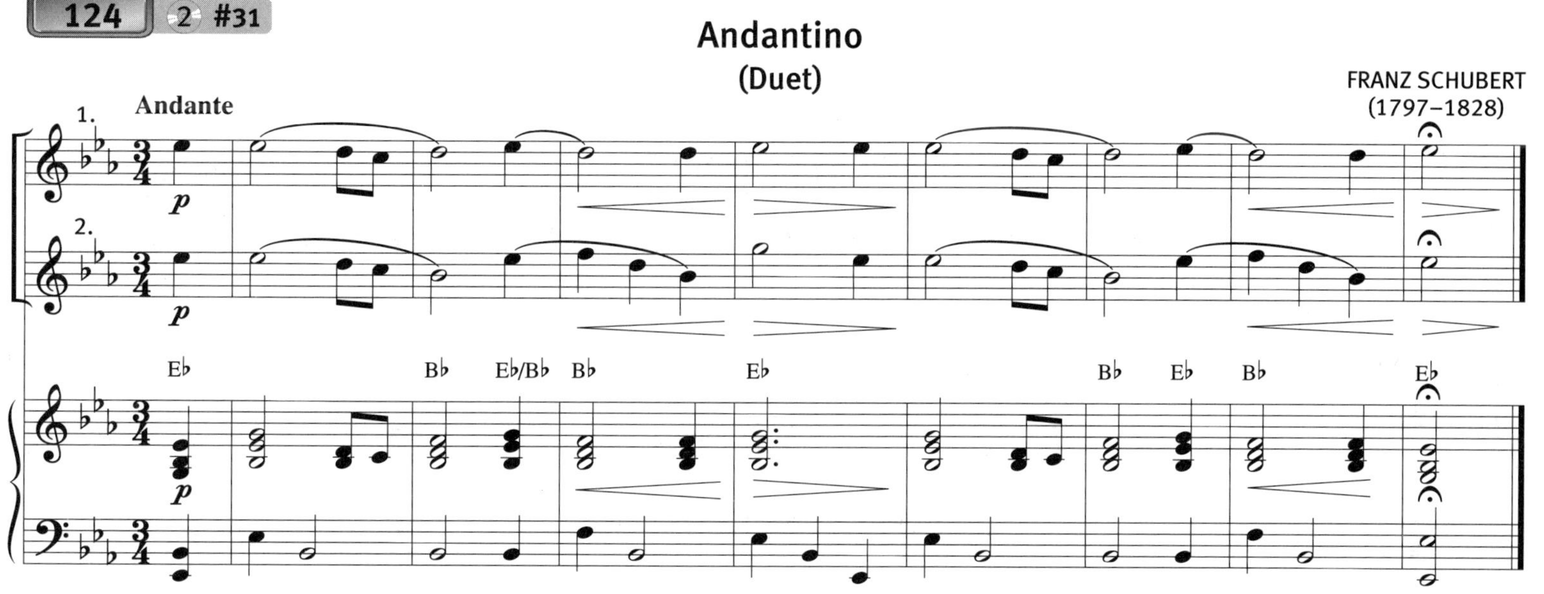

125 2 #32

Working Up

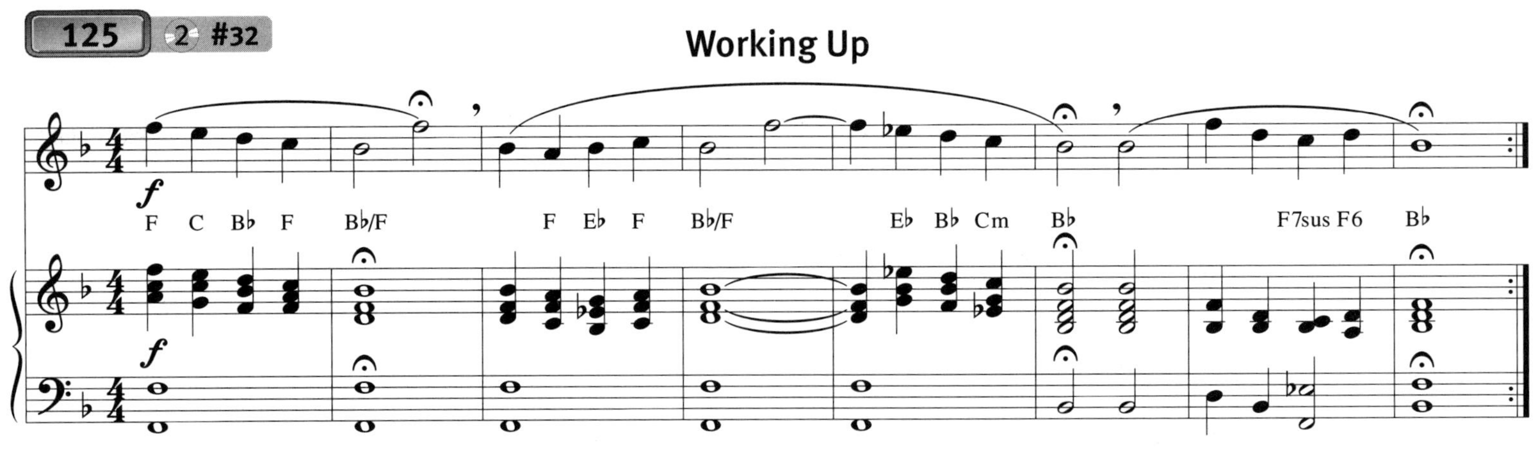

126 2 #33

Expanding the Range

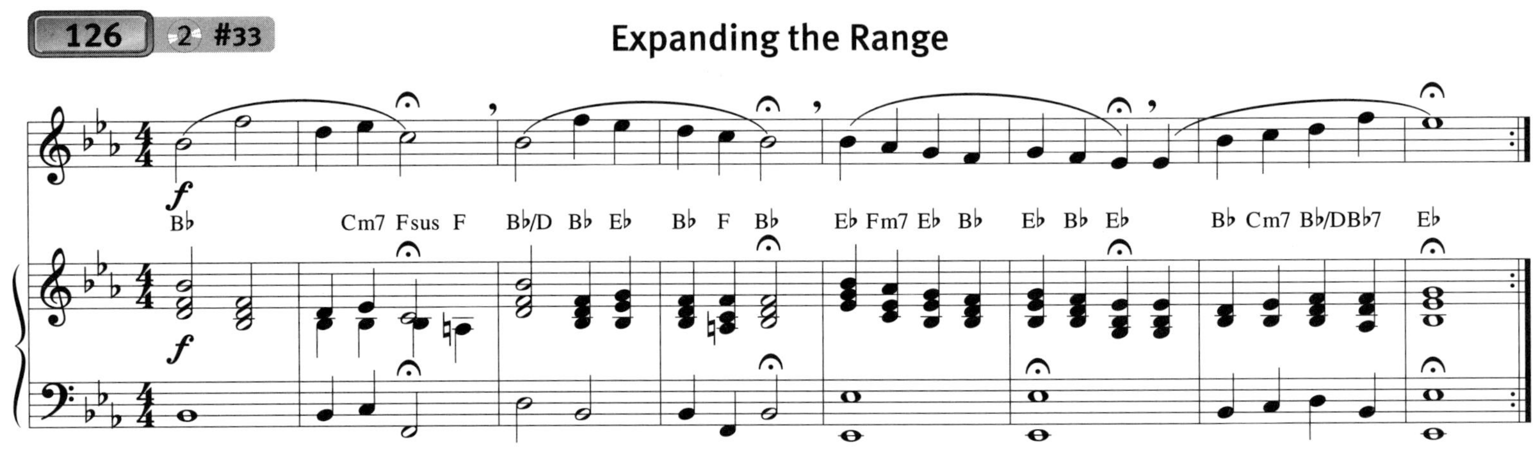

127 2 #34

Anvil Chorus
from *Il Trovatore*

GIUSEPPE VERDI
(1813–1901)

128 2 #35

Hey, Ho! Nobody's Home
(Round)

Hungarian Folk Song

129 2 #36 Divisi Rock

SANDY FELDSTEIN & LARRY CLARK
(b. 1940) (b. 1963)

Allegro
div.
unis.
div.
unis.
div.
unis.
div.
f
Bb Eb/Bb Bb Cm7 Bb F Bb F7 Bb/F F7 Bb/F F Bb Eb/Bb Bb Cm7 Bb Eb Bb F7 Bb
f

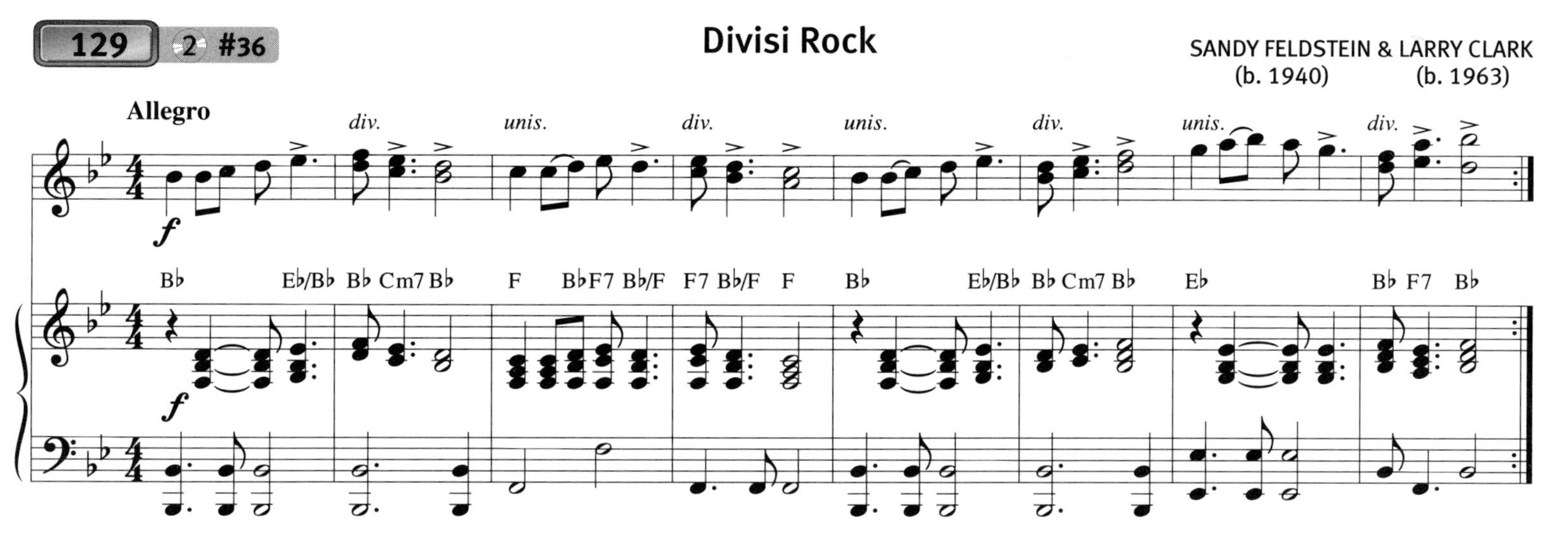

131 2 #38 Largo

from the *New World Symphony*

(Duet)

ANTONÍN DVOŘÁK
(1841–1904)

Largo
1.
2.
p
Bb Cm7/Bb Bb F/Bb Bb F7 Bb/F F
f
p
Bb Cm7/Bb Bb F7 Bb/F F7 Bb

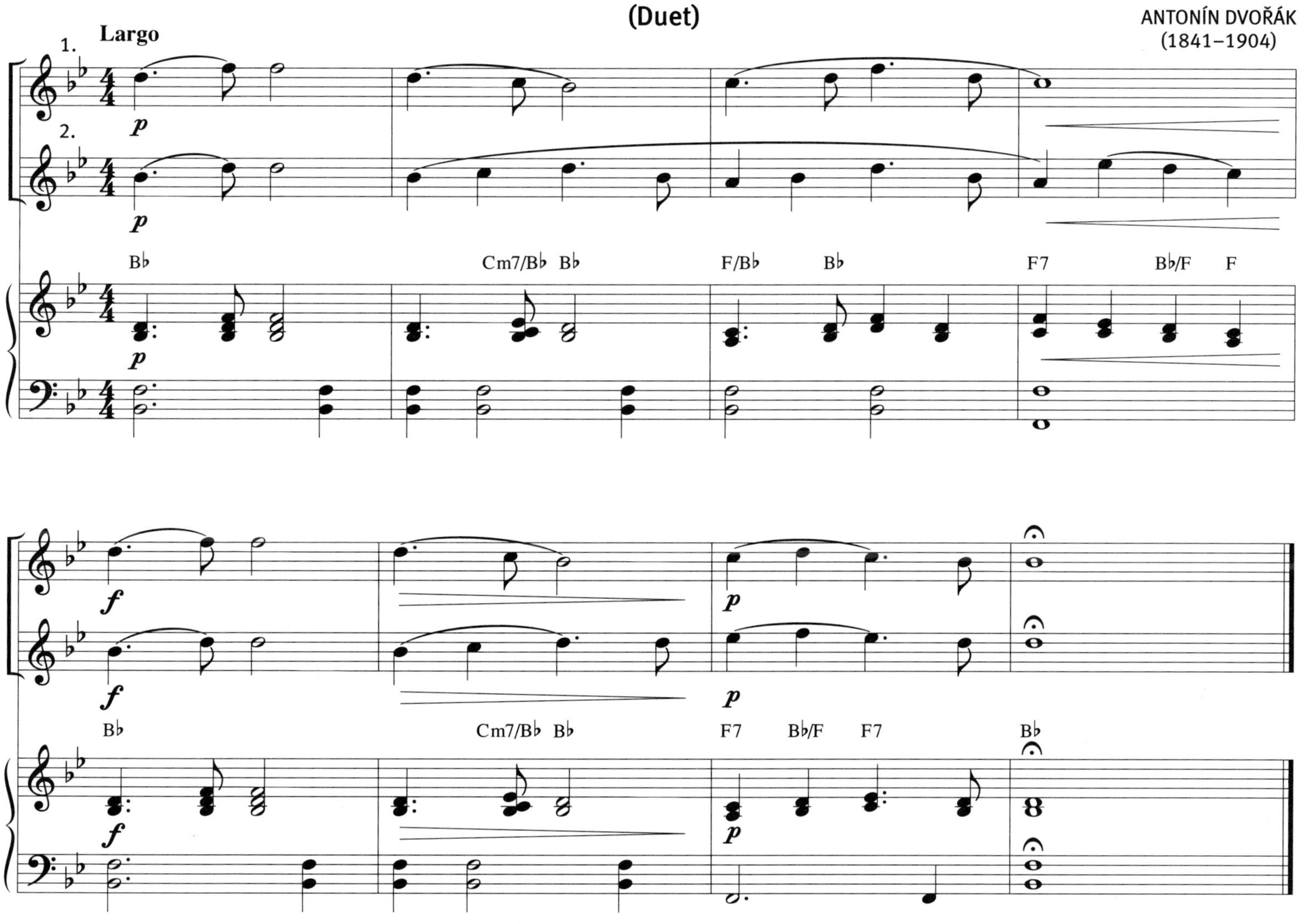

132
2 #39
Tallis Canon Chorale
THOMAS TALLIS
(1510–85)
Andante
Eb Bbsus Bb Cm7 Eb/G Fm/Ab Fm/Bb Eb Eb/Bb Fm7 D°/F Eb Fm/Eb Bb7/D Eb Eb/G
Ab Bb Eb Fm Bb/D Eb Ab Bb7/Ab Cm7 Eb/G Fm7/Ab Bb7 Eb
rit.
133
2 #40
Scale Study
F C F F Bb F Bb/F C F Bb(b5)Bb F/A Gm7 F Gm7 F
134
2 #41
Ode to Joy
from Symphony No. 9
LUDWIG van BEETHOVEN
(1770–1827)
Moderato
legato
Bb F7sus/C Bb/D Cm7 Bb F/A Gm Eb Bb/F F Bb F7sus/C Bb/D Cm7 Bb F/A
Fine
D.S. al Fine
Gm Eb Bb/F F Bb F Bb/F F Bb/F F Bb/F D7/F# Gm C7 Fsus F

135 2 #42
Dreydl, Dreydl
Allegro
Chanukah Song
mf
mp
B♭
F Gm7 F/A F
136 2 #43
The Duck
Moderato
Chinese Folk Song
mp
mf
E♭
B♭/D E♭
B♭5 E♭
f
E♭
B♭ E♭
rit.
137 2 #44
ADVANTAGE
COMPOSITION/IMPROVISATION
Cm9
138 2 #45
Happy Little Donkey
(Round)
American Folk Song
A.
Andante
B.
C.
F7 B♭
F7 B♭
Fsus7 B♭

139 2 #46
Sliding on Up
Largo
mf
Bb F Eb Bb Cm Bb F Bb/F F Bb/F F
Bb Eb/Bb Bb F7 Bb/D Cm/Eb Bb/D F/C Bb
140 2 #47
In a Minor Mode
Andante
mf
Dm Gm/D Em7(b5) A7(b9) Dm Gm Em7(b5) A7(b9) Dm Dm
1. 2.
rit.
141 2 #48
Sakura
Japanese Folk Song
Andante
p
mp
Gm Dm7 Gm Dm7 Gm F Gm Cm7 Gm Cm
Gm F Gm Dm Gm Dm N.C. Dm
mf
rit.

142
2 #49
Cielito Lindo
Mexican Folk Song
Allegro
Eb
Eb+
Ab
C7/G
Fm7
Bb9
Ab/Bb
Eb
Eb6
C7/E
Fm7
Bb9
Eb
Eb
144
2 #51
Night Song
(Duet)
ROBERT SCHUMANN
(1810–56)
Andante
legato
legato
Eb
Bb7/D
Bb
Eb
Ab
Bb
Cm
Fm/Ab
Bb
Ab/C
Bb/D
Bb
legato
Eb
Bb7
Ab
Eb
Ab
Bb
C
Fm/Ab
Ab
Bb
Eb

145 2 #52

Chorale

CARL MARIA von WEBER
(1786–1826)

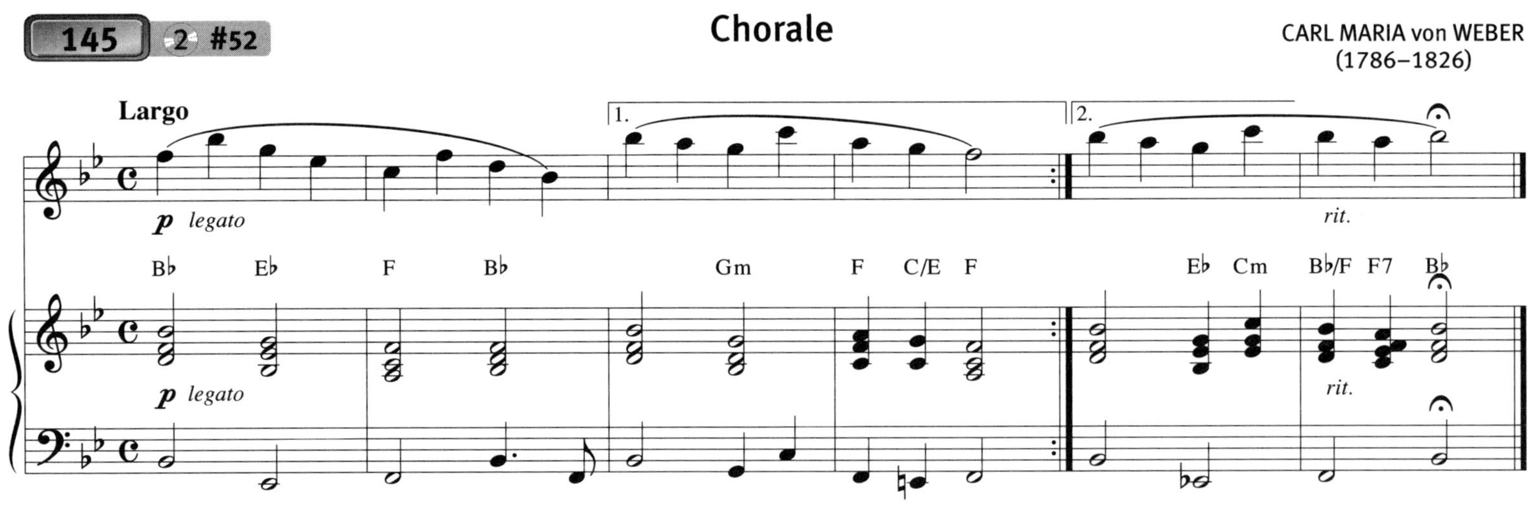

146 2 #53

All on the Right

147 2 #54

A New Jingle

JAMES PIERPONT
(1822–93)

148 2 #55

Kum Ba Yah

African Folk Song

Eb
Ab
Eb
Ab/Eb
Eb
Bb7
Eb
Ab/Eb
Eb
rit.
149
2 #56
Ach! Du Lieber Augustine
Allegro
German Folk Song
Eb
Bb/D
Eb
Bb/D
Bb
Eb
150
2 #57
ADVANTAGE
MUSICIANSHIP · Streets of Laredo
Allegro
Moderato
Andante
Largo
American Folk Song
rit.
mp
F(9)
Gm7/C
F(9)
Gm7/C
F(9)
Gm7
F(9)/C
C7
F(9)
151
2 #58
See the Conquering Hero
from Judas Maccabaeus
(Duet)
GEORGE FRIDERIC HANDEL
(1685–1759)
Moderato
1.
2.
Bb
F
F7
Bb
F
Bb
Bb/D
F7
Bb

152 2 #59
Kopprasch Study
GEORG KOPPRASCH (ca. 1800–33)
Allegro
153 2 #60
Swing Low, Sweet Chariot
American Spiritual
Andante
mp legato
154 2 #61
Minuet
JOHANN SEBASTIAN BACH (1685–1750)
Moderato
rit.
155 2 #62
Bonjour, Mes Amis
Cajun Folk Song
Allegro

Bb
Eb
Bb/D
Cm7
Bb
Bb7
Eb
156
2 #63
ADVANTAGE
COMPOSITION/IMPROVISATION
Using any notes from the Bb Major scale and rhythms you know, improvise or compose your own melody.
Cm7 throughout
157
2 #64
Dona Nobis Pacem
(Round)
A.
Andante
Traditional Canon
mp legato
Eb
Bb7
Eb
Bb
Cm7
Bbsus Bb
Ab
Eb/G
Eb
Bb
Eb
mp legato
B.
Bb/D
Eb/G Bb7sus/F Eb
Bb/D
Ab
Eb/G
Bb/D
Eb
C.
Bb7
Eb
Bb7
Ab
Eb/G
Bb7
Eb

158 (2) #65

Hymn of Thanksgiving

Netherlands Folk Hymn

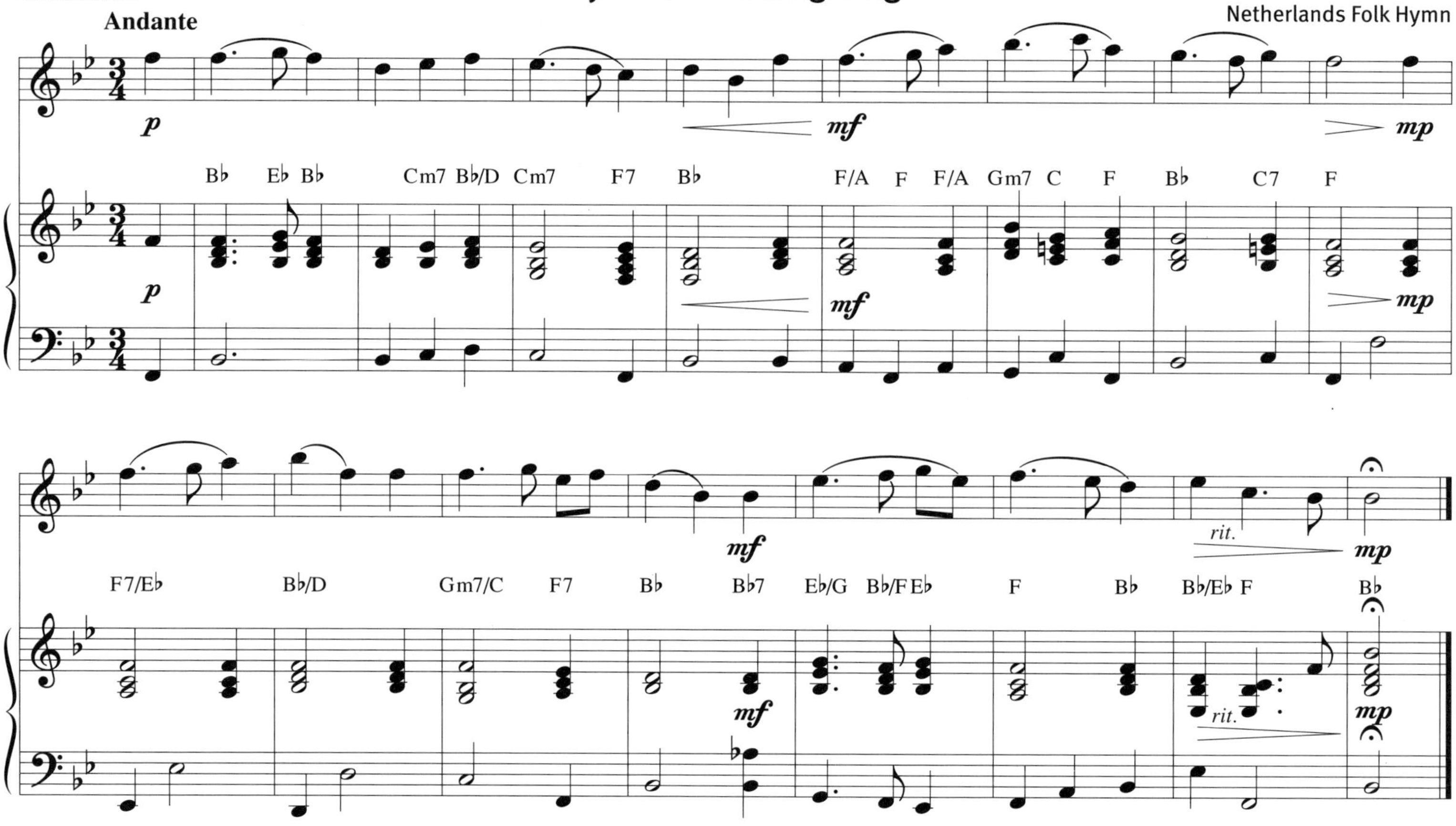

Andante

p *mf* *mp*

Bb Eb Bb Cm7 Bb/D Cm7 F7 Bb F/A F F/A Gm7 C F Bb C7 F

F7/Eb Bb/D Gm7/C F7 Bb Bb7 Eb/G Bb/F Eb F Bb Bb/Eb F Bb

mf *rit.* *mp*

159 (2) #66

Wagner Technique Study

ERNEST F. WAGNER
(ca. 1870–1954)

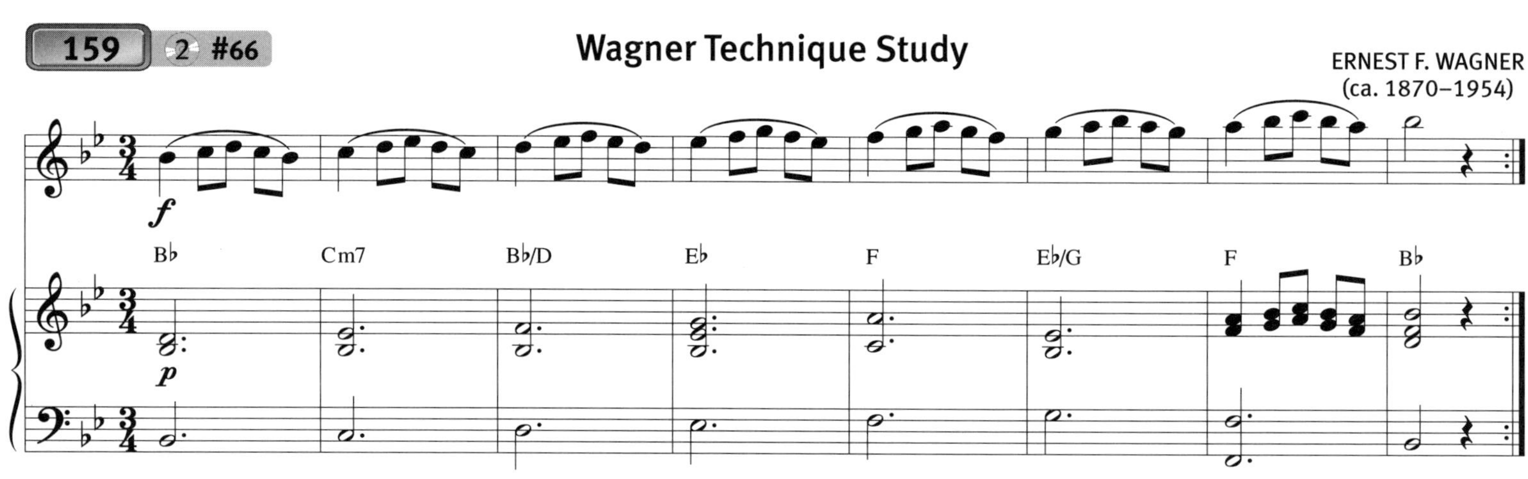

160 (2) #67

Austrian Hymn

FRANZ JOSEPH HAYDN
(1732–1809)

161 2 #68

Minuet

WOLFGANG AMADEUS MOZART (1756–91)

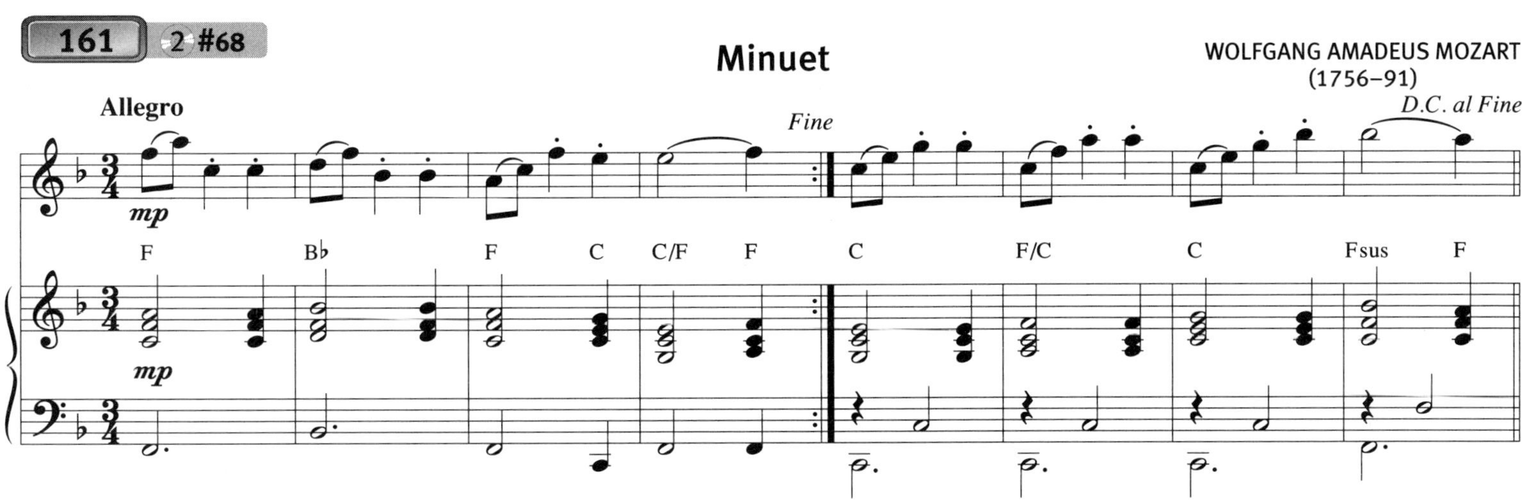

162 2 #69

ADVANTAGE PLAY BY EAR · **Michael Row the Boat Ashore**

163 2 #70

Make New Friends
(Round)

American Camping Song

164 2 #71

Amazing Grace

American Folk Song

Largo

mp f

E♭ Fm7 E♭/G E♭9 A♭ E♭/G Fm7 E♭ Fm7 E♭ Fm7 B♭ Cm7 B♭/D

mp

E♭ Gm7(♭5) A♭ E♭/G Cm Am7(♭5) Fm7/A♭ Fm7/B♭ E♭ E♭/G Fm7 E♭

f mp rit.

165 2 #72

Marine's Hymn

Traditional

Allegro

mf

Fine 1.

B♭ F7 B♭ F7 B♭

mf

2.

D.S. al Fine

f

E♭ B♭ E♭ F Gm F°/A♭ F/A

f

166 2 #73

Auld Lang Syne

Scottish Folk Song

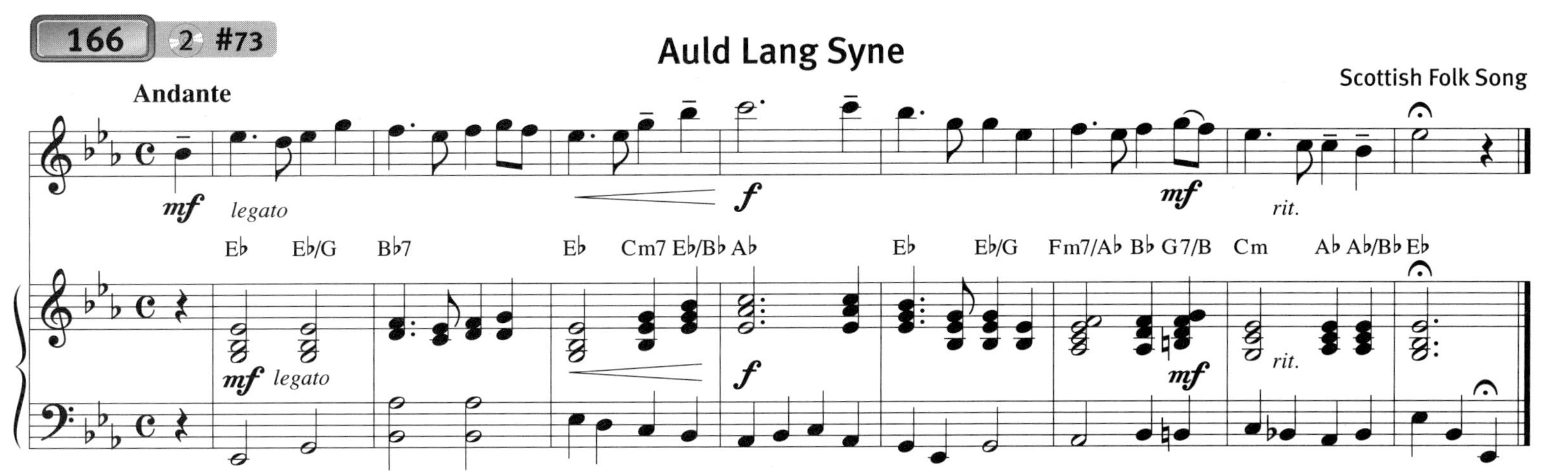

168 2 #75

Alleluia
(Round)

WOLFGANG AMADEUS MOZART
(1756–91)

A. Allegro

mf

E♭ Fm B♭ E♭ Fm B♭7 E♭

mf

B.

Fm B♭ E♭ Fm B♭7 E♭

C.

Fm B♭ E♭ Fm B♭7 E♭

ADVANTAGE 2 #79

SOLO PERFORMANCE

FOR FLUTE, CLARINET, ALTO SAXOPHONE

Jupiter
from *The Planets*

GUSTAV HOLST
(1874–1934)

28
29
30
31
32
33
34
35
36
37
38
39
mf
40
41
mf
42
43
f
44
45
46
rit.
Allegro
47
48
f
rit.
49
50
51
52
53
54
55
56

ADVANTAGE 2 #80

SOLO PERFORMANCE

FOR TRUMPET, TROMBONE, BARITONE AND TUBA

The Ash Grove

Welsh Folk Song

27
28
29
30
31
32
33
mp
mf
34
35
36
37
38
39
40
p
41
42
43
44
45
46
mf
mp
47
48
49
50
51
52
53
rit.
rit.

ADVANTAGE 2 #81

SOLO PERFORMANCE

FOR OBOE, ALTO CLARINET, BASS CLARINET, TENOR SAXOPHONE, BARITONE SAXOPHONE, HORN

23
24
25
26
27
28
p
p
29
30
31
32
33
34
f
mp
L.H.
f
mp
35
36
37
38
39
40
p
mf
p
41
42
43
44
45
46
47
mf
mp

ADVANTAGE 2 #82

SOLO PERFORMANCE

KEYBOARD PERCUSSION

mf
f
mf
f
mf
mf
f
f

ADVANTAGE
2 #83
SOLO PERFORMANCE
SNARE DRUM/BASS DRUM
Sonatina
MUZIO CLEMENTI
(1752–1832)
Allegro
Snare Drum
Bass Drum
Piano
on rim

R L R R L R L L
18
19
20
21
22
23
24
mf
25
26
27
28
f
29
30
5
31
32
9
ff
33
mf
34
ff
35
36
37
38

ADVANTAGE 2 #83

SOLO PERFORMANCE

ACCESSORY PERCUSSION

18
19
20
21
22
23
To Timp.
Timp.
24
mf
25
26
27
28
To Tamb.
f
Tamb.
29
30
31
32
33
mf
ff
34
35
36
37
38

ADVANTAGE PERFORMANCE 1 #78

Genesis

SANDY FELDSTEIN & LARRY CLARK
(b. 1940) (b.1963)

C2 E♭M7 B♭2 C2 B♭2 C2 E♭M7 C2 E♭M7
30 31 32 33
C2 E♭M7 B♭2 C2 B♭2 C2 E♭M7 C2 E♭M7
34 35 36 37
C2 E♭M7 B♭2 C2 B♭2 C2 E♭M7 C2 E♭M7 C2 E♭M7
38 39 40 41 42
44
B♭2 C2 Cm B♭2 A♭2 Gm7 Cm B♭2 A♭M7 Gm7 Cm B♭2 A♭2
f
43 44 45 46 47 48
Gm7 A♭2 Gm7 E♭/F A♭/E♭ B♭/D C2 B♭2 A♭M7(♭5) A♭M7/G B♭/F
49 50 51 52 53 54
59
N.C. 2 Cm B♭2 A♭2 Gm7 Cm B♭2 A♭M9 Gm7
mp 2 f
55 56 57 59 60 61 62
Cm B♭2 A♭2 Gm7 A♭2 B♭2 A♭2 Gm7 Cm B♭2 A♭2 Gm7 A♭2 Gm7 E♭/F A♭/E♭ B♭/D
63 64 65 66
C Gm7(♯5) C Gm7(♯5) C
67 68 69 70 71 72

THE YAMAHA ADVANTAGE™

Musicianship from Day One

Also available in this series:

Conductor Score	YBM101
Flute	YBM102
Oboe	YBM103
Clarinet	YBM104
Alto Clarinet	YBM105
Bass Clarinet	YBM106
Bassoon	YBM107
Alto Saxophone	YBM108
Tenor Saxophone	YBM109
Baritone Saxophone	YBM110
Trumpet	YBM111
Horn	YBM112
Trombone	YBM113
Baritone B.C.	YBM114
Baritone T.C.	YBM115
Tuba	YBM116
Keyboard Percussion	YBM117
Percussion (Snare Drum, Bass Drum)	YBM118
Combined Percussion	YBM119
Accessory Percussion / Timpani	YBM120
CD Accompaniments (2 discs)	YBM122

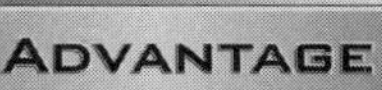

www.yamahaadvantage.com  **Extra activities and teaching aids available online, free of charge;**

- Lesson plans
- Music history lessons
- Programming ideas
- Letters to parents, music advocacy
- Extra exercises for students
- Play along tracks, games, quizzes, assessment exercises
- Student rewards
- Master classes, online forums
- E-mail access to authors